Entrepreneur Extraordinaire

Top experts share their secrets to business success

THRIVE Publishing
A Division of PowerDynamics Publishing, Inc.
San Francisco, California
www.thrivebooks.com

ISBN: 978-0-9850828-3-3

Library of Congress Control Number: 2001012345

Printed in the United States of America on acid-free paper.

■ ■ ■

We dedicate this book to you

the entrepreneur, business owner, sales professional or consultant, whether you are experienced or are just starting out on your path to entrepreneurship. You recognize the power of knowing what to do, as well as how and when to do it in order to be wildly successful. We salute you for wanting more knowledge designed to advance your business—and we celebrate your commitment to being the best you can be. We are here to give you all we have to make your entrepreneurial venture extraordinary.

The Co-Authors of *Entrepreneur Extraordinaire*

Table of Contents

Acknowledgements

Gratitude is an important part of business success. Before we share our wisdom and experience with you, we have a few people to thank for turning our vision for this book into a reality.

This book is the brilliant concept of Caterina Rando, the founder of Thrive Publishing™ and a respected business speaker and strategist. Without Caterina's "take action" spirit, her positive attitude and her commitment to excellence, you would not be reading this book, of which we are all so proud.

Additionally, a truly dedicated team has worked diligently to put together the best possible book for you and supported all of our efforts. We are grateful for everyone's stellar contribution.

To Patricia Haddock, whose experience in copywriting and copyediting proved invaluable, and whose magic pen and expertise ensured that this book would be the best it could be.

To Tammy Tribble, Barbara McDonald, Tricia Principe and Noël Voskuil, our designers extraordinaire, who brought their creative talents to the cover and book layout, thank you all for your enthusiasm, problem solving and attention to detail throughout this project.

To our exceptional proofreaders, Simone Martel, Tony Lloyd and Rua Necaise, thank you for ensuring we dotted all the i's, crossed all the t's and placed every comma where it belongs.

We also acknowledge each other for delivering outstanding information, guidance and advice to you. Through our work in this book and with our clients, we are truly committed to enhancing the success of women entrepreneurs throughout the world. We are truly grateful that we get to do work that we love and contribute to so many in the process. We do not take our good fortune lightly. We are clear in our mission—to make a genuine contribution to you, the reader. Thank you for granting us this extraordinary opportunity.

The Co-Authors of *Entrepreneur Extraordinaire*

Introduction

Congratulations! You have opened an incredible resource, packed with great ideas that will enhance your entrepreneurial experience in ways you cannot yet imagine. You are about to discover how to strengthen and develop your business skills to ensure that your business is profitable, sustainable and thriving.

Your success comes as the result of more than talent, commitment and hard work. Your success will also be determined by how well you manage all aspects of your business. When you are an entrepreneur, you are responsible for everything—marketing, product development, customer service, sales and networking. Every success and setback you experience will come from the decisions you make. Your success as an entrepreneur depends on how productively and effectively you run your business and how well you communicate and cultivate customer relationships and strategic alliances.

We know you want to be the absolute best entrepreneur you can be. With this book, you will quickly learn how successful entrepreneurs get the very best results. As top experts in each of our respective specialties, we have joined to give you the most powerful information and strategies available.

Each of us has seen how even small changes can transform and uplift a business. Here is just a sample of the benefits you will find inside to transform yours:

- Communicate your personal brand and make it part of everything you do.
- Overcome setbacks and emerge stronger than before.
- Get control over your time, paperwork and email.
- Maximize the social networks and the Internet to grow your business.
- And much more!

All the entrepreneurs you will meet in this book want you to succeed. We have outlined for you our top strategies and included the most expert advice we have to advance your success.

To get the most out of *Entrepreneur Extraordinaire*, we recommend you read it once, cover to cover, then go back and follow the advice that applies to you in the chapters most relevant to your current situation. Every improvement you make will increase your confidence and effectiveness and positively affect how others respond to your business.

Just learning what to do will not create transformation. Take action and apply the strategies, tips and tactics we share in these pages, and you will reap many rewards. With our knowledge and your action, we are confident that, like our thousands of satisfied clients, you too will benefit from *Entrepreneur Extraordinaire*.

To your unlimited success!

The Co-Authors of *Entrepreneur Extraordinaire*

Why Ethics in Business Matters!

By Nilda Perez

The twenty-first century has brought change—some good, and some not so good. Changes in technology have taken the world by storm and brought the world closer. Sudden rapid changes in the economy have caused stress and distrust. In fact, I believe the level of distrust shown toward our leaders is unprecedented. I believe that leaders who do not keep their word and withhold information have contributed to employees and customers feeling devalued and disrespected. A leader's word is no longer valid. We look to lawyers to validate what was once sealed with just a handshake.

There are no black-and-white answers. Ethics takes us into gray areas that are not clear and may not seem as if they would make a huge difference. However, the little foxes spoil the vineyard! Over time, what seems like small, not-so-bad choices can damage a business beyond repair and harm both employees and clients. The effect is cumulative!

At a time when nothing appears secure, you can safeguard against damaging your business and hurting your employees, customers and reputation. How?

You can perform in one of two ways. You can:

1. Exercise courageous leadership and exemplify integrity or
2. Do what is convenient without considering others

"Have the courage to say no. Have the courage to face the truth. Do the right thing because it is right. These are the magic keys to living your life with integrity."
—W. Clement Stone, American author

Leading your business with integrity takes courage. Dr. Bruce Winston, Regent University's dean of the school of Global Leadership and Entrepreneurship, states that a quintessential leader is one who leads through *agápao*. A leader who leads through *agápao* love is one who does the right thing at the right time for the right reason, one who loves in the social and moral sense. Leading with high moral values can only be obtained through *agápao* love leadership optimized through servant leadership. Servant leadership is the framework for integrity.

Leading with integrity is not always easy. Often, you have to take the high road and turn down opportunities that will give your business quick results. It is critical to take into account that the results you want are long term. A proverb I live by is, "A good name is more desired than great wealth, favor is better than silver or gold," *Proverbs 22:1*.

Your integrity is the most valuable thing you can own and maintaining integrity takes courage. According to Brigadier General Dr. John H.

Johns, who served as a combat arms officer in the Army, honesty and loyalty are values that are the ingredients of integrity. Honesty and loyalty are relative terms that are employed selectively when convenient. This does not negate the fact that there are individuals who are honorable, honest, loyal and of great integrity, and these individual's success will have longevity. Although this is true in every aspect of life, it is most essential in business.

This pragmatic stance to do what is convenient for you as the leader or for the organization over what is right is born from a lack of courage and conviction. Over time, it will become evident and both your clients and your staff will lose faith in your product or service. It takes tenacious courage to be authentic and lead with integrity despite the hardships it may bring to the organization. The sphere of doing what is right over what is convenient will pay high dividends if the choice is right over pragmatic.

Compromising Values in a Changing World

"We must become the change we seek in the world."
—Mohandas Gandhi, Indian political and ideological leader

Nicolas Mauro, a professor of management at Dowling College in Oakdale, New York, argues that ethics is a reflection of the character of an individual or organization. Defining an ethical code about what is right or wrong manifests in the business practices. You, as the leader, set the tone for the direction in which your business goes. The single most important thing in any business's culture is its value system that is formulated from the leaders—your value system. As the leader, your values determine the culture of the business. Google® is a prime example of how leaders value creativity, ingenuity and innovation. As a result, they have established an environment that is relaxed, fun and friendly. They have chosen creativity over experience. These leaders have fostered a happy atmosphere to allow their staffs' creative juices to flow. Things that you will see in the Google workspace are:

- Local expressions of each location showcasing that region and personality, from a mural in Buenos Aires to ski gondolas in Zurich.
- Bicycles or scooters for efficient travel between meetings, dogs, lava lamps, massage chairs, large inflatable balls
- Googlers sharing cubes, yurts, huddle rooms and a few solo offices.
- Laptops everywhere—standard issue for mobile coding, email on the go and note-taking.
- Foosball, pool tables, volleyball courts, assorted video games, pianos, ping pong tables, and gyms that offer yoga and dance classes.
- Grassroots employee groups for all interests, like meditation, film, wine-tasting and salsa dancing.
- Healthy lunches and dinners for all staff at a variety of cafés.
- Break rooms packed with a variety of snacks and drinks to keep Googlers going.

Adopting the concept of values vs. culture, I began to evaluate my values and the culture I wanted to be the thumbprint of my business. I questioned how my vision would be interpreted. I came up with three things that are at the core of my value system. A business that 1) embodies integrity, 2) deposits wisdom and stimulates greatness and, 3) delivers every message through a spiritual infrastructure. As a result, the physical as well as personal environment permeate these values. Integrity is evident in every business transaction, considering both the client and the staff. Through training, coaching and consulting, wisdom is directing clients toward realizing their goals. The infrastructure of every activity is navigated through spiritual origin.

You determine how your business operates, how the vision and mission are formulated and how daily operations are conducted. This all comes directly from your value system. What is important and valuable to you is what will resonate throughout your organization. This is the heartbeat of your business—evaluating it is critical.

Warren Bennis, an organizational consultant, author and pioneer in contemporary leadership studies, believes that it is necessary to "know thyself," meaning separating who you are and who you want to be from what the world thinks you are and wants you to be. The greatest leaders possess self-awareness. They lead with precision, and therefore, their businesses are fruitful. If you adopt this mindset, your business will thrive.

How Are Values the Heartbeat of Your Business?

When there is a problem in a business, the leader's values are not often identified as the pressing issue behind the problem. Because values are often subconscious and perceived as personal and separate from the decisions we make in life, no one links values with the possible cause of problems in business. So, let's discuss how values impact the status quo of a business.

As you have read, every single decision made in a business is based on the leader's value system. When a leader puts people before profit, the result is a happy employee environment. Employees will feel valued and considered, and it will be evident in how they do their jobs. There will be less conflict and more productivity. Often, we think that being well versed and knowledgeable about our products or services is what brings value to our employees and customers. While this is important, true value is the integrity we exemplify—and integrity can only come from our core values.

There is a proverb that states, "Honesty guides good people, dishonesty destroys treacherous people." Loyalty, honesty, respect, truthfulness, kindness, hard work and doing the right thing because the right thing is not always easy increase your value.

When a leader does not have integrity, he or she can lose value overnight. One crooked deal, one dishonest word can destroy a person's and a business's reputation—just that fast.

Is There a Good and a Right?

Is there a good and a right? Theorists such as John Dewey, Charles Taylor and William James believe in a pragmatic system of good and right. They theorize that there is no real authority for what is good and right and that each individual decides what is right for them based on their personal worldview. This supports the assumption that character or conduct should be practical or convenient for the individual without considering the other. I believe this theory is a recipe for disaster. It takes tenacious courage to be authentic and lead with integrity, despite the hardships it may bring to the individual and the organization.

What about the Gray Areas?

Ethical dilemmas seem to rest primarily in the gray areas. Clearly, black-and-white right and wrongs are easier to determine—the gray areas, not so much.

According to John G. Bruhn, PhD, provost, dean and professor of sociology at Penn State University in State College, PA, writing in the *Journal of Business Ethics*, "All organizations have gray areas where the border between right and wrong behavior is blurred, but where a major part of organizational decision-making takes place." He argues, "Gray areas become problematic when leaders, by their own inattention, inaction and poor modeling, minimize the importance of building a moral community by delegating gray area issues to second-tier administrators. Gray areas provide wiggle room in coping with ethical dilemmas in organizations."

The problem with the gray areas is this: You have a lack of defined boundaries that allow issues to be left open to interpretation. This increases the possibility of doing the wrong thing. Often, business decisions must be resolved on a case-by-case basis—there is no absolute right or wrong. In these cases, you have to use discernment to make the right decision. Having keen perception and the ability to make correct judgments constitutes discernment. According to Bruhn, the areas where the right and wrong border are blurred are where major decision-making occurs.

Some gray areas are common when boundaries are loose or completely lacking. Boundaries come in several forms and may be physical, social, psychological and emotional. They can come from policies, procedures, rules or formal or informal agreements. If any of these areas are open for interpretation, they become gray areas. The more rigid the boundary, the more competition it instills that keeps people and issues separate. Flexible boundaries foster cooperation, teams, partnerships and inter-departmental problem solving. Loose or undefined boundaries can at some point allow unethical practices in an organization. These boundaries must be identified and addressed immediately in order to maintain the high standards of integrity.

Does Integrity Exist?

Integrity is a lot broader than just honesty and ethical standards. It also includes the approach employees take toward every aspect of their jobs. This comes from you and your leadership team exemplifying integrity in all areas of your business. Anything short of the truth is a lie—when you are not truthful in every area of business, you lose integrity. This is a sure way to create a dysfunctional business.

This is the way to do business, and your employees will mimic these values as long as you model them. Clients and customers will feel the impact through the value given them in the products and services.

The gray areas matter to those on the receiving end who may be impacted or hurt by a careless leader who focuses solely on doing what is pragmatic, convenient and self-serving. Doing the right thing for the right reason is servant leadership and can be transformational. A value system needs to always consider the well-being of others.

In a world that perceives pragmatism as the road to success, doing the right and ethical thing may seem foolish. It takes enormous courage to lead with integrity, stand firm, be authentic, have conviction, lead through influence yet consider others and always do the right thing because it is the right thing to do.

As the Leader Goes, So Goes the Organization

Aubrey Malphurs, founder of The Malphurs Group, coined this statement, "As the leadership goes, so goes the organization." At its core, the definition of leadership is influence. Good leadership influences people. Bad leadership also influences people.

I encourage you to immerse yourself in understanding your clientele's and your employees' pain, and address each accordingly. Change comes from a transformational leadership mindset. Keep in mind that you, as the leader in your business, are focused on piloting the culture of the business. What you do will be continually observed and mimicked. Exhibit loyalty and trustworthiness, and value your employees equally as much as your clients, and it will resonate throughout your business. This, combined with integrity, will make all of the difference in how your business will develop.

Ethics in business *does* matter. As a leader in your organization, you set the tone in the significance that integrity will have in your environment. Even if there have been times when you have given in on those gray areas, you can begin today to change the culture in your business and to have the courage to make the changes necessary for flawless ethical standards.

Nilda Perez

Aspire 4 Life,
Coaching and Consulting Services

(845) 206-4602
www.Aspire4Business.com
nilda@Aspire4Life.com

Nilda Perez is the CEO and president of Aspire 4 Life Coaching and Consulting, established in 2004. She consults with businesses, not-for-profit organizations, churches, ministries and groups and gives them concrete strategies on how to efficiently lead and grow their organizations. She assists individuals to start their own businesses and consults with small businesses in devising strategic plans to achieve the greatest productivity with ease.

A published author, noted speaker and widely read blogger, Nilda holds a bachelor of science in social science from Adelphi University, a masters in clinical social work from Fordham University and is currently a doctoral candidate in global leadership and entrepreneurship at Regent University, Virginia Beach, Virginia.

Nilda has upper management positions in several organizations. While running her therapy and coaching business, which qualifies her to train, coach and speak, Nilda speaks, consults and trains in management, business and leadership. She is a native New Yorker, born and raised in the Bronx, and she went through the public school system. In 1999, she relocated to the New York Hudson Valley.

■ ■ ■

Journey to the Future

Effectively Take Your Company from "Here" to "There"

By Cynthia Bruno, Esq.

If you wanted to travel in your car from your current location to a new destination, whether that took you across town or across country, you would most likely log in to the software mapping application of your preference and plug in the addresses of your current location and your desired endpoint. Your search query would respond with a map showing you visually the highlighted route, alternate route options, step-by-step instructions on how to get from "Point A" to "Point B" of your selected route, including mileage and distance of each step and, finally, total distance and estimated time to travel the route. It would also include the choice to select between shortest time and shortest distance, as well as the option to avoid certain roadways, such as highways and toll bridges, which may contribute to a more enjoyable journey. This information attests to the fact that "the shortest distance between two points is a straight line," and there is also more than one route from A to B.

Now, instead of a car ride, you are an extraordinary entrepreneur desiring to take your business from "Point A" to "Point B." While it isn't quite as simple as inputing addresses into a computer, by utilizing a bit of forethought and organization and defining clearly your end point and interim objectives, you can arrive at "Point B" every bit as effectively as if you were following computerized map guidance.

The first step is to define where "there" is—in other words, where do you want to go or what do you want to achieve?

Once you know where you're headed, you can then develop the objectives and milestones required to achieve your desired outcome. In order to understand clearly the desired "Point B," you first need to create a clearly identified mission and vision. These 5,000-foot-level concepts keep you focused when operating at ground level as dictated by everyday life.

"The shortest distance between two points assumes you know where you're going."
—Robert Brault, American author

Mission

What is the ultimate purpose of your venture or what do you want to be when you grow up?

A mission statement defines the fundamental purpose for your company. It is akin to the question asked repeatedly of us as children: "What do you want to be when you grow up?" A mission statement is the target for which one continually strives, which is ever fully achieved. It is defined by an action word that summarizes the company or organization's primary purpose or greater good. It focuses on a higher purpose and not one that is centered around making money.

As a personal example, at Hume Global Enterprises, we work in the agricultural industry. Our mission is "to aid the agricultural industry internationally to sow seeds of success in the cultivation of healthy, affordable and abundant products for the world to enjoy." Accordingly, all of our business efforts are focused on furthering this goal, and all business decisions are measured for their consistency with this purpose.

Here are some examples of mission statements from the public websites of major organizations with my emphasis in italics:

- National Public Radio®: "The mission of NPR is *to work* in partnership with member stations *to create* a more informed public—one challenged and invigorated by a deeper understanding and appreciation of events, ideas and cultures."
- Target®: "Our mission is to make Target the preferred shopping destination for our guests *by delivering* outstanding value, continuous innovation and an exceptional guest experience *by consistently fulfilling* our Expect More. Pay Less.® brand promise."
- Ben & Jerry's® product mission: "*To make, distribute and sell* the finest quality ice cream and euphoric concoctions with a continued commitment to *incorporating* wholesome, natural ingredients and *promoting* business practices that respect the Earth and the Environment."

When you can define the ultimate purpose for your business, product and service, you have defined your mission.

Vision

What actionable goal do you desire to achieve in order to realize your mission?

As the name suggests, a vision captures the image of what you want to achieve as opposed to the mission that defines the greater purpose for which you want to be known. A vision must be objective, tangible, specific, clear and attainable. It is the image in your mind when you close your eyes and dream about what you desire to accomplish. A vision speaks to how you will work to achieve your mission in the near future.

A vision should reflect the primary goal for one to five years and may change beyond that as your business evolves, achieves goals and responds to a changing environment. A vision is "Point B" in the mapping software analogy. It is the "there" to which your company is headed from the "here" where you presently stand.

"Good business leaders create a vision, articulate the vision, passionately own the vision, and relentlessly drive it to completion."
—Jack Welch, American executive and
former CEO of General Electric®

By way of example, presently at Hume Global Enterprises, our product is the Hume Seed Finder. It is our vision in the next five years to sell Hume Seed Finders internationally in the majority of countries engaging in modern agricultural processing while defining ourselves by an unparalleled commitment to customer service, quality and excellence. When we achieve this vision, we will have acted in furtherance of our mission to aid the agricultural industry at an international level.

Although still broad and non-specific in nature, our vision is achievable and measurable. In monitoring sales over time, we will understand how closely we have achieved our sales goals and whether we have done so consistent with satisfied customers, product quality and our own standards of excellence. Other examples of vision statements taken from their public websites include:

- Whole Foods®: "Our motto—Whole Foods, Whole People, Whole Planet—emphasizes that our vision reaches far beyond just being a food retailer. Our success in fulfilling our vision is measured by customer satisfaction, Team Member excellence and happiness, return on capital investment, improvement in the state of the environment, and local and larger community support."
- Cheesecake Factory®: "Through a shared commitment to excellence, we are dedicated to the uncompromising quality of our food, service, people and profit, while taking exceptional care of our guests and staff. We will continuously strive to surpass our own accomplishment and be recognized as a leader in our industry."

In these examples, there are identifiable criteria from which each company can evaluate how well their operations support their vision. Once you identify the big picture you plan to achieve, you have your vision and know where you are going. The next step is to figure out how to get there.

Objectives

Objectives are the major steps of your road map.

"Plan backwards as well as forward. Set objectives and trace back to see how to achieve them. You may find that no path can get you there. Plan forward to see where your steps will take you, which may not be clear or intuitive."

—Donald Rumsfeld, American, former secretary of defense of the United States

With our computerized mapping program, when we input "Destination A," "Destination B" and select "get directions," it will return each of the steps we need to take in between. It often begins with something along the lines of "start out traveling east on Main Street for two miles" and proceeds from there, identifying each step of the journey and the distance you must travel. So too with your business, you must identify the steps you must take from your current position to achieve your vision. No longer at the 5,000-foot level, objectives are specific, actionable and measurable. They are also not so overly specific as to be "down in the weeds."

Objectives identify the major steps, outline what you need to achieve and define the time you're allotting to it. They do not necessarily include any specificity as to the methodology for achieving this step.

Numerous objectives support achieving a vision. Each objective is the equivalent of telling you that you need to get from here to the corner and that it will take you approximately five minutes to accomplish this. It does not define whether you are going on foot, in a car or by bike, nor does it tell you along which lane of traffic or side of the street you should proceed. Unlike mapping software that requires you to complete the first step before taking the next, it is possible to follow more than one objective simultaneously in pursuit of the same focus.

Using a real-world example at Hume Global Enterprises, I mentioned our vision involves expanding sales of our Hume Seed Finder around the globe and in the majority of countries practicing modern agriculture. Our objectives, therefore, identify the countries where we want to target our marketing and networking efforts and the priority for doing so. We also envision ourselves performing at the highest levels of customer satisfaction, quality and excellence. As you would guess, we have objectives to achieve production quality, volume and efficiency. We will execute our performance objectives simultaneously with existing sales while working on our sales objectives for growth in order to achieve our vision.

- What are the major steps you need to take with your business to achieve your vision?
- Do they involve your sales, production, performance or, more realistically, some combination of all the above?
- What is the priority order you assign to each of your major steps being mindful to prioritize the "need" to do items before the "want" to do items?
- How long do you think it will actually take to complete each step?

Breaking down the journey into an outline of its component parts is critical to achieve success and render the process more manageable.

Milestones

The devil is in the details.

"The secret of success is to do the common things uncommonly well."
—John D. Rockefeller, American financier

If you remember creating an outline for a high school English composition, the subject matter of the paper is akin to the business mission, the paper's thesis is the vision, the topic sentence of each paragraph is your objective and the bullet points supporting each paragraph are the milestones.

Milestones lay out in detail all of the baby steps you need to take to achieve your objectives and realize your vision. They are the routine tasks associated with every business and guide day-to-day focus to keep your company moving in the right direction.

Milestones support the objective in getting from your starting point to the corner. At Hume Global, the milestones supporting our objective to conduct business in countries around the world include the following specific to each country or region targeted:

- Trade shows in which to participate in order to make contacts and market our product.
- Organizations to join.
- Companies to approach via direct and indirect marketing efforts.
- Networking opportunities to pursue.

Outlining your milestones drives the plan of action for the month, the week and even the day. It identifies the priorities for each milestone based on the scheduled dates and allocated timeframes associated with the various opportunities. For example, if one trade show or conference identified for participation is three months sooner than another, preparing for the first conference takes priority.

Milestones are "down-in-the-weeds" actions from which you generate your operating "to-do" lists. Because many entrepreneurs are big picture visionaries, identifying the actions to take on this level of detail may prove challenging and the least enjoyable of the activities discussed in this chapter. Taking the time to identify and prioritize milestones in support of your objectives, however, is critical to maintaining focus and ultimately achieving success.

"Above all, you want to create something you are proud of. That's always been my philosophy of business. I can honestly say that I have never gone into any business purely to make money. If that is the sole motive, then I believe you are better off doing nothing."
—Sir Richard Branson, British founder of Virgin Group®

As an entrepreneur, you possess the necessary idealism to sell a product or provide a service for a greater good. Taking the time to identify your mission, vision, objectives and milestones will help ensure the focus necessary now and in the future to achieve that purpose. Initially, you may have financial constraints that require you to serve as a "jack-of-all trades," quickly identifying the tasks associated with achieving your objectives and milestones that aren't conducive to your natural strengths—hiring others to perform those tasks is critical to your sanity and your long-term success. See "Hiring the Right People" by Cynthia Fassler on page 217.

Commit to writing your high-level mission and vision and immediate company objectives to unite others on your team, such as employees, contractors and consultants. Finally, solidifying these principles specific to your business will take you from an ordinary entrepreneur to an extraordinary entrepreneur.

Cynthia Bruno, Esq.

Hume Global Enterprises

Helping sow seeds of success

(559) 593-1471
cynthia@humeglobalenteprises.com
www.humeglobalenterprises.com

When Cynthia Bruno, chief executive officer of Hume Global Enterprises, graduated from UCLA School of Law and began her professional career as a JAG Officer in the U.S. Navy, she had no idea that the professional opportunities in her future would provide her a diverse forum from which to understand organizational effectiveness and keys to success. Throughout her 16-year career in the military, national security arena and as a corporate executive, Cynthia learned the attributes, principles and practices that contribute directly to the success of a program or company.

In 2011, following nearly seven years as the chief operating officer, chief financial officer and general counsel for a real-estate development firm, Cynthia joined Hume Global Enterprises as the chief executive officer. Cynthia's responsibilities include defining key corporate concepts in order to organize and grow Hume Global from a small family business centered around sales of one product to an international company focused on marketing tools within the agricultural industry.

With her education and extensive professional background in military, government and private companies, Cynthia has a diverse array of talents and experience. Her specialties include fostering organizational effectiveness, developing strategies to enhance corporate performance and achieving results.

■ ■ ■

Selecting Your Best Business Model

By Karen Terry, CLC

A business model officially defines the core aspects of a business, including the purpose of the business, its offerings (products and services), strategies, infrastructure and organizational structure, trading practices, and all operational processes and policies.

In other words, it's the way in which you or your company operates on a day-to-day basis in order to generate revenue, income and profits. A business model exemplifies exactly how a business works in order to make money.

Business models differ slightly from business plans in that business plans are formal written documents outlining the day-to-day operations as well as the long-term goals and vision for a company. Usually, business plans are written during the conceptual phase of the business, whereas business models describe or reference businesses that are already up and running. Details of the business model and how a business operates should be part of a business plan, but typically, a business model is the business plan in action.

Successful Business Models

So how do companies make their money? Let's look at some business models of successful businesses. First, let's look at some larger corporations from a couple of established industries.

Computer software companies, such as Microsoft®, make and sell software that runs primarily on a desktop computer. You probably use their popular suite of products, which includes such staples as MS Word®, Excel®, PowerPoint®, Access® and Outlook®. In this model, the customer pays for the product one time, and then pays to upgrade their software to a new version every few years. In addition, many programs are sold with an annual maintenance agreement, which may include technical support and an automatic upgrade to the latest version of the software when it is released. Therefore, software companies make their money from selling software, upgrades, and from annual maintenance fees.

Fast food restaurants make money selling food to you, the consumer. This is known as the direct sales model. They make their money from selling a product, which could be tacos, hamburgers or pizza. Their food is tasty, and people are hungry, so these businesses have historically been very successful. Now these businesses have a lot of competition—in other words, there are many restaurants that sell pizzas and hamburgers, so they can't raise their prices very much.

So what do they do to make money?

When a customer places an order at a fast food restaurant, most likely they will be asked, "Do you want fries with that?" The reason these restaurants push fries (and soft drinks, breadsticks, etc.), is because these "extras" have a huge profit margin. In other words, these businesses make most of their money from selling those items.

Both software and fast food companies sell a product directly to an end user or a consumer. Another type of business model is called a "business-to-business" model, such as B2B, intermediaries or wholesalers. In this model, businesses sell primarily to other businesses. A few examples are companies that manufacture components sold directly to manufacturers, specialized training classes only offered to corporations, wholesale office supplies, and oil service companies who sell equipment directly to oil and gas companies rather than to the public.

Traditional Business Models

So if you are a small business, sole proprietor, entrepreneur or individual service professional, what types of business models are there for you?

Hours for Dollars. One of the oldest and most well-known business models is known as the "hours for dollars" model. This is where one hour's worth of time is equivalent to a certain amount of money. If you charge by the hour for your expertise (as many sole proprietors do), then you are trading your time for money. Historically, the "hours for dollars" business model was used by service professionals— attorneys, engineers and accountants who charged by the hour for their time spent working on a case, project, or tax return. In addition, many businesses use this model to pay their employees a certain wage for each hour worked.

Selling Products by Direct Sales. Now let's examine the direct sales model. This is where a business sells products— in the form of tangible goods— directly to customers, and the customer is paying for an item instead of time. How do you make money in a direct sales model?

A small business can sell toys, food, office supplies or any other consumer good. In this case, merchandise is usually purchased from a supplier at a set amount (known as "cost" or the wholesale price), and then resellers mark it up. Many sole proprietors and entrepreneurs create their own products to sell—in the form of books, e-books, home study courses on CDs or DVDs, etc. The retail price is the difference between the markup and the wholesale price. Once expenses are factored in, any net gain the reseller makes is profit they can keep.

If goods are sold from a brick-and-mortar store, then the amount of money that can be made is more limited, because a store is only open during certain business hours. Contrast that to online retailers, where sales can be made from an Internet website around the clock. It is a different business model!

Leveraged Business Model. In this business model, a business capitalizes on the work of others. Normally this is done by hiring employees or using contractors. If you are self-employed, and you can't perform the work yourself, you can hire a contractor to do it for you, pay them and keep a percentage of the total fee for yourself. Business owners profit because employees are doing the work for them.

Leveraging the work of other people is the concept and strength behind network and multi-level marketing (MLM). If you can get other people to sell a product for you, then you can keep a percentage of the sales they make. The more people you have under you (and the more under them) selling your product or service (known as your "downline"), the more money you will make.

Another version of the leveraged business model is agencies. An agency is a business that represents clients for the purpose of getting them business and jobs, while keeping a percentage of the revenue from that job. Temp, training, and talent agencies operate this way. A client or business comes to the agency with a certain need, be it a temporary worker, a corporate trainer, or an actor/model, and the agency meets that need by matching them with a human resource on their staff or in their network. Many freelancers, service professionals and sole proprietors work with agencies because it can be a steady source of jobs and referrals.

Franchises. Another option you may want to consider is a franchise business. A franchise is a "turnkey" system for an entrepreneur who does not want to start a business from scratch. You buy an established brand, and then implement the company's existing business model, including all systems and processes. You get the benefit of a recognizable name as well as a successful model. There are even companies out there that help you decide which franchise is right for you!

Picking the Business Model for You

So how do you know which business model is the right fit for you? Well, there are a couple of things you need to do first. The first thing is to select your target market. Whom are you going to sell to? Your market will determine whether you are going to sell products or services (or a mix of both). The third thing is to determine your delivery method. In other words, how will your product or service be delivered? If you are going to sell consumer goods, will you open a store or a website (or both)? If you are going to offer coaching as a service, will your coaching be provided in person, on the phone, or via Skype?

What you select as your business model (how you will work) is one of the single most important decisions that you will make in your business! There are advantages and disadvantages to all business models. Most professional service providers start charging by the hour, but eventually become frustrated when they experience a limit on the amount of money they can make.

Because the number of hours in a day, week, month, and year are already set, the "hours for dollars" model imposes an artificial cap on your income. There are only so many hours that you can actually bill your client. If you go up on your hourly rate to make more money, some clients will not want to pay that rate and you will lose them! Another drawback to the "hours for dollars" model is that if you are not working, you are not actually earning any money (this is a concept known as active vs. passive—or residual—income).

For these reasons, there has been a shift in the professional world away from the "hours for dollars" model to selling packages. A "packaged product" is a bundle of services that is sold for a certain amount of money. Therefore, instead of charging by the hour to do an income tax return, a CPA might package that service along with other services, such as filing quarterly tax statements, all for a set price. A web designer might create a package that includes the most common tasks performed when setting up a new website. Packages are gaining popularity because it provides a way to charge based on the value and results provided to the client, rather than an hourly rate.

You have to find what works for you. It may be a combination of offering products and services. There are pros and cons to each method. Products can provide a continual stream of income to supplement your active income. However, there are some disadvantages to selling products as well, including potentially small profit margins, and having to purchase products up front.

One thing you need to know about business models is that they are constantly changing. How you make money today will not necessarily be how you make it ten years from now. Periodically, you will need to evaluate your existing business model and look for ways you can improve, innovate and adapt. This may be via improving processes, applying new technology, or finding better ways of doing something.

Innovation

Innovation is critical in business. Sometimes a new business model completely revolutionizes a particular industry. Why? A business looked at the old model and came up with something that was better or more efficient.

A prime example is Dell Computer, Inc. Dell is one of the most successful high-tech companies because of their direct business model. At the time that Dell entered the computer market, most computers had already been built and were sitting in stores waiting to be bought. This means that excess inventory collected on shelves during slow times and quickly became outdated.

Dell turned this model on its head by not building a computer until a customer ordered it. Dell sells the computer directly to the end user (vs. a store), which has several advantages. Dell is able to cut costs by cutting out the intermediary, and because they sell inventory over the Internet, they eliminate the high overhead associated with a retail store. Customers love it because the computer is made to a customer's specifications and delivered within a few days.

Another example is Southwest Airlines (SWA). Before Southwest entered the market, air travel was considered a luxury. When SWA entered the airline business in 1971, they had a different philosophy. They offered low fares, snacks (peanuts) instead of full meals, open seating (vs. assigned), and short hops instead of long-haul flights. They also operate out of smaller alternative airports, thereby saving on landing and departure fees. In short, they were the "no frills" airline, and they became very successful because their business model was completely different from other airlines at the time. Southwest made air travel affordable and brought the ability to fly to the masses. Along the way, they forced other airlines to adapt!

However, even with all of these innovations, nothing in the last century has changed existing business models more than the Internet!

Microsoft's business model selling software worked well for years. Now, new software applications (apps) run on mobile devices. In many cases, consumers can download apps free directly off the Internet instead of paying hundreds or even thousands of dollars for a single software package. Google®, historically known as a search engine, now offers free email, which cuts into Microsoft's market share. This means that Microsoft and other traditional software companies have to find a way to adapt to changing consumer expectations and new business models in order to stay competitive.

Innovation is one of the most critical factors to having a long-term successful business. Businesses that don't ever change, innovate, evolve or keep up with the times don't grow and thus won't have a future. If you are a sole-proprietor, you must keep up with the latest and greatest technology, constantly improve your processes and periodically reinvent yourself and your business. If you keep on doing the same thing repeatedly, in the same way, and don't ever come up with anything fresh or new, you will stagnate and eventually go out of business. Other companies with newer business models will pass you by.

So what can you do to innovate?

Never let yourself get stagnant. Be flexible and open to new ideas. Learn as much as you can, attend industry conferences, and keep up with trends and technology. Figure out ways to apply new technology to your existing business processes. Know what your competitors are doing. Diversify your client base and have multiple revenue streams. If you are a sole proprietor, you can do this by mixing up your offerings and selling products in the form of home-study courses, packages, products and services.

Constantly add new products and services to your offerings and find new ways to make money. Think of all the ways businesses make money—for instance, they charge fees for everything! (Note: I am not condoning fees, but I am suggesting you get creative about new ways to bring in income.) Look for passive income and partnering opportunities. It may benefit you to own your own building or real estate. I know one dentist who owns his own building and rents out space to the orthodontist and other specialists when they come to see his patients! This is a very smart business model that provides an extra stream of revenue for his practice.

Business models are dynamic. Learn to recognize signs of change in your market. Your existing business model may become obsolete if you can't adapt to the market quickly when it starts to change. Then you won't be in business very long! Innovation is the key to success. I wish you much success, in business and in life!

Karen Terry, CLC

Certified Life Coach,
Certified Technical Trainer

(281) 826-3656
www.fulltimewoman.com
kcsterry@gmail.com

Karen Terry is a business, career and life coach based in Houston, Texas. She helps women, working moms who have had enough of the corporate world, and stay-at-home moms who want to transition into the world of entrepreneurship.

Karen works professionally with women and men on all kinds of career issues, including those who are starting new businesses, choosing or changing a career, seeking work and life balance, handling retirement issues around starting a second career or business, and reaching the next level in a career. Her clients see results in all of these areas because she offers a unique step-by-step program for change in combination with general life-coaching skills. She truly loves helping her clients change their lives for the better!

As a busy woman and mom herself, Karen had a successful training business for 12 years before becoming a coach. She is a top-rated instructor and trainer, professional speaker and award-winning writer and blogger. Her second book, *Full-Time Woman, Part-Time Career,* CMS Press in 2005, won an Axiom Business Book Award in 2008.

■ ■ ■

Going Global with Ease and Grace

Expand Your Business Exponentially and Make It a Big Vacation!

By Dakota McKenzie

Are you a natural leader? Are you a visionary, powered by amazing insights and inspired by possibilities you can see before others? Have you seen it all, done it all, built up your business to where you never thought you could?

What is next?

Have you thoroughly defined the essence of what you do? Have you done this recently? Have you done this on a very deep level, so that there really is only one of you—so you are unique?

I want you to do this because when you do, you will be able to take the essence of your offering and put it into a potent group training, book or certification program that spreads your work exponentially, even worldwide.

I also want you to learn a mindset, emotional skillset and lifestyle that will help you hold the biggest expansion possible with grace and ease and create your life as if you are always on vacation.

You know what it feels like when it's time to start on a new voyage and set out through uncharted waters with a pocketful of vision, a few maps and a big, in-progress plan. You get antsy and feel pressured, as if there is not enough room to breathe in the life you have created. You are being compressed, not because your world is changing but because you are getting too big for it!

You need to spread your wings and fly, not once, but repeatedly in your life and your business. Learning to do this when you are a beginner is exciting and challenging. Learning to do it all over again after you have become an expert in your field is even more exciting and challenging. You have to master this humble process and learn to welcome it time and time again. When you do so, your business and your life will take you to amazing places. You will live your life to the fullest and create transformational effects in others and in this world that you cannot dream of.

"In the beginner's mind there are many possibilities, but in the expert's there are few."
—Shunryo Suzuki, Japanese Zen master

Welcome Beginner's Mind

Beginner's mind is the natural next step upon achieving mastery. It opens the way to a new journey toward a new level of mastery.

Beginner's mind, however, can be a very scary place for experts, especially experts who have not yet experienced the whole cycle of mastery followed by beginner's mind followed by a higher-level mastery.

It can be a liberating experience to practice beginner's mind. When the responsibility of being an expert is lifted, you can see more clearly what's around you. You are open to moments of unmitigated brilliance. If you have been carrying the role of expert for a while, it can be a big relief to swing the wheel in the other direction. It can even feel like a vacation.

Sometimes, you need a guide to help you navigate unfamiliar territory. A guide can help you on the passage through beginner's mind. Your guide is someone who:

- **Provides support and affirmation.** They see and believe in you and your creation.
- **Is experienced and inquisitive.** They ask the questions that help you become big and proud and create amazing things.
- **Makes you accountable.** They use a strong and loving hand when you try to make excuses, back off, give up, disappear.
- **Makes it fun!** Fun equals clients, money, success, fame and all that good stuff. It is one of the top things that make life worthwhile!
- **Holds the vision.** Their job is to hold your vision and clarify it until you become strong enough to hold it yourself.

Exponential Expansion with Ease and Grace

Are you ready to take off your expert's garb and set out on an exciting and fun journey to a completely new level of depth, fulfillment, ease and mastery?

This process can be applied to any area in which you want to expand. I use it to create group or certification programs and help people find their energetic power type in the system I created, *Your Sacred Hand*.

The nuts-and-bolts are a one-size-fits-all recipe.

- **Ask the right questions.** There is an art to asking questions that open both the left and right sides of the brain and get you started on the journey with all your resources. Are you feeling the way you want to feel in your life and business? When you imagine feeling the way you want to feel, who and what shows up connected to that? Who are your clients? What are you doing with them? How are you doing it?

- **Explore freely where you are drawn.** Use tools to explore that bring both sides of the brain into the process, and your heart as well, while encouraging complete freedom. Let your questions become *quests, leading you deeper into your own journey.* On my website, I provide powerful guided meditations and other tools for this that you can use to take your own personal journeys. You can learn to do this yourself too. Go deeper into the quest-ions. Where are you? What are you smelling? Hearing? Seeing? What have you learned about yourself and your possibilities?

- **Find a new treasure.** Let yourself get excited like a little kid when you find something truly fantastic that belongs to you and is waiting to get out. Yay! Now you have opened a new world for yourself inside your head about who you can be and how you can feel. Wow! Set a time of day to visit it, every day! For example, Jack loves to fly and knows those moments in the air connect him with the business vision he is creating. However, he does not have time to get out and do it often. He has created a collection of YouTube® videos that remind him of some of his "high moments" flying. He gets back to his computer five minutes early from lunch every day and watches these to juice himself up with his higher purpose and *the way it feels to him before he goes into the rest of his client day.*

Just five minutes a day can change the course of your life.

Pilots flying need to make very small and frequent corrections to their trajectory due to the rotation of the earth—otherwise, they would end up in Ft Lauderdale, Florida, instead of New York City. Five minutes a day can make the difference between alligators or the Big Apple!

- **Bring it home and look at old stuff with new eyes.** Bring that treasure into your life and let it enlighten everything else. You may get some amazing insights that free up things that previously felt stuck. You may find everything else is brushed with the magic dust of this new thing. You may find that this new thing becomes the main attraction.

  Allow yourself to simply notice what is changing. This is important and worth repeating. Ask yourself: "What is changing in my life?" Post this on your fridge: How is my life different this month than last month due to my five daily minutes of course correction? Post a big blank piece of paper on your fridge next to this and write "What's New" at the top in capital letters. At the end of each month, write a few sentences about all the things that have changed and where this is leading you. Refresh the paper as necessary and keep the pages. You may want to do quarterly reviews. When you have finished reviewing "What's New," find some fantastic new way to celebrate.

Right now, think of all the things that are limiting you. Write them in your mind. Make the biggest ones bright red and the lesser ones pink or yellow.

There. How was that? You may have found some limiting factors you did not know you had, and you may have written some you now realize are not really limiting you. Now, take a vanishing marker and erase all the yellow and pink ones, then all the red ones.

You are now starting with a blank page. No limiting factors.

Starting tomorrow morning, what does your life look like? Just imagine it or write this on a piece of paper if you like. You may have done this exercise before. Do it again with no limits. You have all the time in the world, all the love in the world, all the money in the world and all the clarity in the world. Most importantly, allow yourself the state of beginner's mind and approach the picture of your own life with completely fresh eyes. Let new answers come.

Now emblazon this picture in your mind on a big gold award certificate. You have won! This is your life. How do you feel? Let that feeling imprint itself deeply into you. That is your navigational device for this journey.

Lianna has made a special name for herself as a talented videographer who creates brilliant marketing videos. She is the proud creator of a one-of-a-kind VIP day that is a growth experience in itself like no other. Even though she is in demand at events and retreats, she feels in competition with other gifted, up-and-coming videographers who charge much less than she does. She feels compressed by a sense of competitiveness. She is also pressed for time and not sure what the next step is to expand her business.

What Lianna needs to do is expand her vision to fit her true self. Because she started as a videographer, she sees this as her identity, so she competes with other videographers in her mind. Since this is what she holds in her mind, it makes its way into her marketing and self-presentation and becomes her reality. She has a gift she has only partially discovered that has nothing to do with video. Video just happens to be the current tool she is using to share it. Notice that her greatest pride and delight is her special VIP day, which has its own process and just happens to be carried out through video.

Lianna needs to go through a transformational doorway to the very core of who she is and discover her unique gift in its raw form without videography. How can she expand her VIP program without the video component? Only then will her real essence shine through as never before, whether she stays behind her camera or ventures into other fields. A world of possibilities opens up. She herself will be one-of-a-kind and can create her VIP day with or without video. She may even expand it into a special training and certify others to teach it. The competition, in other words, could become her very own followers.

Erina's ideal life includes more time, more freedom, more self-expression, more money, more influence. She has a heart-based, one-on-one practice with high-end clients, runs an online group program, does live events and hosts retreats. She loves what she does. However, she does not love being as busy as she is becoming. She wants to write a book about a system she is developing that helps people grow personally as they better understand how to market their work. The only time she can find to write her book is during her family vacation.

Erina needs to find ways to duplicate herself so that she has more of herself for herself. How to do this? She could look at her time drains and create programs that carry her work forward without her presence. Every aspect of her practice could benefit from this. She could create online materials for her group program, VIP days for her high-end clients, group VIP mastermind days, and could train and certify assistants to share her work.

If she were able to implement even some of these changes, she could take a family vacation and a month or two off to write her book. Her business could be expanding without her!

The doorway she needs to go through to implement this expansion goes to the core of what she is about and further defines her work through the process of formatting it into programs and certifications that have her special quality but can be delivered by other people. She needs to make her work so crystal clear that she can delegate it without worrying that it will lose its power.

What do these amazingly gifted women have in common at this point in their lives and businesses? They have a pressing need to find a way to do more with less. This need requires that they get extreme clarity about their gifts and how those gifts are delivered to the world.

They need to hone their gift down to its very simple essence, which can be translated across time and space while staying true. They need to get so clear about who they are that it goes into everything they create, naturally and without effort.

Leverage Yourself with Ease—Do More With Less

The only way to consistently do more with less is to make your offering so potent and so representative of the essence of your gift that it can be dropped anywhere in the world, picked up by someone else and still share its intrinsic value.

With full potency, you can create products, trainings, certification programs and books that give people the real value they would experience from your work in person.

As you can see, achieving full potency means adopting beginner's mind even though you are an expert. You must also go through transformational doorways into the depth of who you are to get an even clearer, stronger, mastery of your one-of-a-kind gift.

"Tell me, what is it you plan to do with your one wild and precious life?"
—Mary Oliver, American poet

The real question is, what are you going to do next with your one wild and precious life? To grow in business and in life you must keep choosing to show up and be as big as you can be. There are others waiting for you and your work, and you may never know all that you mean to them. We stand on and become the shoulders of giants. We need each other. Think of the hundreds or thousands of people you can reach. Think how their lives will be changed.

It is never too late, and your time is now!

Dakota McKenzie

Blissworks! For Business, Unleash Your Bliss Coaching, Discover Your BlissCode

dakota@dakotamckenzie.com
www.dakotamckenzie.com
1 855-BBLOVED

Dakota McKenzie, author, speaker, founder of "Blissworks! For Business," is all about natural power, ease and grace—and a stunningly unique approach that will leverage your business beyond your wildest dreams! She is a spiritual mentor, an entrepreneur extraordinaire and a gifted intuitive rolled into one powerful package.

Since 1995, she's been helping people who help the planet claim their bliss and rock this world and has received downloads from spirit about the most powerful way to help humanity blossom to its full potential. If you are a coach, trainer or entrepreneur who holds a big vision, and you have a hunch to take your product, service or program to lots of people, you can double or triple your income by releasing your amazing gift to the world like an abundant fountain.

Dakota helps you infuse your business with your natural sparkle to magnetize success to create one-of-a-kind products, programs or certification trainings based on your unique teachings and gifts and imbued with your energetic "blissprint." She teaches you how to train and certify others in your program, so your work can grow exponentially and have a big impact on the world.

Intuition—Your Valuable Resource for Immediate Answers for Tangible Business Re$ults

By Susan Rueppel, PhD

Your business has a mind of its own. Would you like to know what it has to say?

Successful business people know that using their intuition provides a powerful business advantage. In today's fast-paced, competitive and often economically challenged business climate, it is important to utilize all the resources at your disposal. Even people who use intuition in their personal life forget to apply it to business in a practical way. Unfortunately, schools and universities rarely provide training on this topic, especially as it relates to business.

Intuition is a valuable and often untapped business resource you can access for expanded creativity, clarity, focus, confidence and more. You can use it to gain a clearer vision, for specific strategies to monetize your ideas and as a roadmap for the quickest path to where you want to be in business.

In several interviews, Oprah Winfrey has stated that two things have made her most successful in business—intuition and timing. For all the major moves in her life, including starting her own television network, she taps into and trusts her intuition and, most importantly, she acts on it. She takes in all the information she can gather and then goes with her gut.

"Learning to trust your instincts, using your intuitive sense of what's best for you, is paramount for any lasting success. I've trusted the still, small voice of intuition my entire life. And the only time I've made mistakes is when I didn't listen."
—Oprah Winfrey, African American media mogul, producer and philanthropist

What is Intuition?

Understanding what intuition is helps us tap into it easier. What if you could learn to tune in and know everything about your business?

In business, intuition is often referred to by names such as "gut instinct," "hunch," "going with your gut," a "hit" and so on. According to *Webster's Encyclopedic Unabridged Dictionary of the English Language Deluxe Edition* published by Gramercy Books in 1996, intuition is the "direct perception of truth, fact, etc., independent of any reasoning process," "a keen and quick insight" and "pure, untaught, non inferential knowledge."

My concept of "business intuition" is using intuition to tap into the truth about business.

Intuition can provide important data that can help with decision making, especially when you have too much data, conflicting data or not enough data. It also helps "connect the dots" in new ways. You can use it as a compass to help you get from where you are to where you want to be in business.

My client, Chris, was considering leaving her corporate job and expanding the business left to her by her father. She wanted to confirm if it was the right move for her and, if so, how to make the transition. Over several intuitive consultations, she gained inspiration, a clearer vision and focus. The insights included an expanded market niche as well as product delivery and partnership potentials. She now has specific, practical and prioritized steps that have her feeling less overwhelmed and more confident about where she is going with the business and how to get there.

People often ask if intuition is a "gift" that only some people are born with. The answer is that we are all born intuitive—sometimes we just forget. In some cases, society conditions it out of us if, as young children, we share intuitive insights that are received with skepticism or even fear. In this environment, we decide that it is not acceptable or safe to be intuitive, and we subsequently often bury or ignore the intuitive messages we receive.

Intuition is not the exclusive domain of women. Men have an equal ability to develop and utilize their intuition, although because of our societal conditioning, men often refer to intuition by other names such as "gut instinct" or "shooting from the hip." Highly successful businesspeople, such as Jack Canfield, Tom Peters and Bill Gates acknowledge using intuition as a key to their success. Many more recent business books also advocate combining logic and intuition for the most optimal vision, strategy and decisions.

Frank came to me looking for ways he could market his wellness products more effectively to help more people be healthier and increase his income. By tuning into his business intuitively, I identified additional market niches, provided clarity around what his customers are looking for and ways to differentiate himself in his field. Specific strategies included creative methods to help customers select the optimal products for their situation, ways to increase repeat business, insights on marketing approach and materials, and partnership profile potential. Frank says that he received ideas for potential market segments he had not thought of and for marketing tools and methods to augment what he had previously done. He said he felt as if he had another partner on board to look at additional ways he might be able to market. This helped him get outside of his own head—that it is like having another pair of eyes.

In business, the focus is predominantly on the left-brain activities of the five physical senses and logic. By incorporating your right-brain intuition, you can become more of a whole-brain thinker, creator and problem solver. All it takes is focused awareness and some practice to access, develop and expand your intuition. Often, we need to pay closer attention to notice and understand the message.

The Intuitive Senses

We are all born six-sensory beings with sight, hearing, touch, taste, smell and intuition. We receive intuitive input constantly. We often forget to pay attention to it, acknowledge it and validate the information we receive.

Intuition is meant to augment our five physical senses, not replace them. Intuition is called also "ESP" or "extrasensory perception" because it provides additional perception for collecting data.

The Four Primary Intuitive Senses. The four primary intuitive senses are extensions of our physical senses and knowing. See the diagram on page 46.

- **Clairvoyance or clear seeing.** This typically appears as images, symbols, pictures or as full motion video as seen with the "inner eyes." People are most familiar with this form of intuition. To engage this intuitive sense, close your eyes and imagine a screen in front of you. This is your intuition screen. Pose questions and ask that you be shown the answers.
- **Clairaudience or clear hearing.** This is hearing with your "inner ear." It can include hearing words, phrases, sentences, full conversations or even music or songs.
- **Clairsentience or clear feeling.** This is when you feel information in your own physical body. Have you ever been around a friend or loved one and suddenly felt discomfort in your body, only to find out they had the same feelings? It refers to being empathic or sensitive to others' thoughts, feelings or emotions. Remember, when it is someone else's discomfort, be aware of whatever they are feeling in their physical body, then let go of the physical distress.
- **Claircognizance or clear knowing.** This occurs when information just "drops in" and you know it while not knowing how you know it. For example, have you ever heard the phone ring and somehow you knew who was calling before you answered, even though the call was not planned? This is how mothers often know to check on their children for no logical reason.

There are two additional intuitive senses people are often not aware of that are extensions of our physical senses: clairalience or clear smelling and clairgustance or clear tasting.

Do you ever smell a particular perfume right before you run into someone who usually wears it and before they actually enter the room? Some people sense a metallic taste when they are around chemicals, such as cleaning products or pesticides even if they are not physically aware of their presence. In business, you may have heard someone say a person or situation "left a bad taste in my mouth."

Using only your physical senses and logic is like seeing the world in black and white. When you add your intuitive senses, it is like seeing the world in Technicolor® and with 3-D® glasses. We all have the ability to develop all our intuitive senses. However, your highest intuitive sense often corresponds to your highest learning mode. If you are a visual learner, clairvoyance may be easiest to recognize and expand. If you are an auditory learner, clairaudience may be easiest. If you are a kinesthetic learner, clairsentience may be easiest.

Below is a diagram of the intuitive senses:

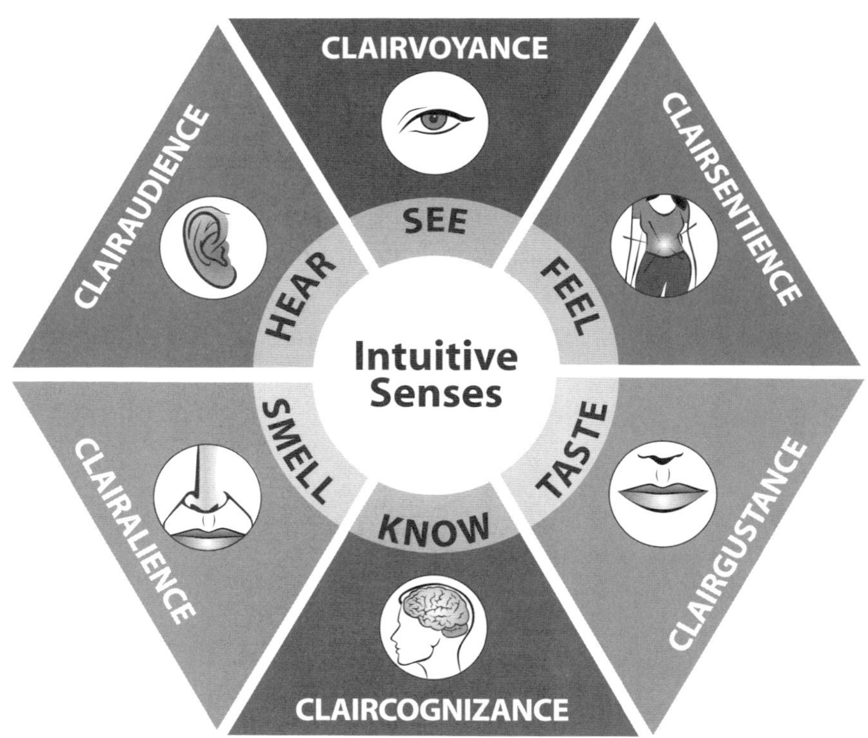

Using Intuition for Business Decisions

Anyone can benefit from more consciously engaging their intuition in business.

- You are thinking about leaving corporate America and are not sure what type of work to do or what type of business to start.
- You are just starting a business and want to know the best use of your time and resources to launch as quickly and easily as possible.
- You have been in business for years and want to expand your products, services, locations and so on.
- You want to resolve challenges you are struggling with.
- You are a "serial-preneur" or "multi-preneur" with several business endeavors and want to get clarity and focus on which of your ideas have the most revenue-generating potential.
- You are a corporate executive who wants a clearer vision for your organization to take into your annual strategic planning process.
- You have people or projects that are struggling, and you want to know why and how to remedy the situation.

In general, intuition can be used in business to gain clarity, make optimal decisions quicker and easier and solve problems. The results are eliminating overwhelm, gaining confidence and a clear path to action. Here are examples of some specific areas of business that can benefit from engaging your intuition:

- Vision and mission alignment and clarity
- Business plan development including strategy and tactics
- Market niche potential
- Knowing what your prospects or clients want
- Products and services potential including packaging
- Marketing, sales and distribution opportunities
- Staff, virtual assistant or referral partner selection
- Prioritizing your time and resources

Clients realize benefits as well. You will discover that when you engage intuition in your business, your clients also benefit from products and services that are in greater alignment with their needs.

As a "multi-preneur" with three very different businesses, Tacye is regularly challenged with how to grow each of her businesses without getting overwhelmed. Working together, she has received prioritized intuitive insights about what her prospects and clients in each business are looking for and detailed, practical marketing and delivery methods to monetize her ideas. She has also gained specifics on systems to put in place to make her processes easy to replicate as her business grows. Just as valuable as the clearer vision and strategies, she now knows how to fan her own inner flame to stay in balance and not get overwhelmed.

Tacye freely admits that she has a propensity to get distracted by what she calls "bright shiny objects" that can range from classes to partnership opportunities. She now uses her newly acquired intuitive skills to focus and determine if an opportunity she is considering will advance her business or is a "bright shiny object." This has saved her lots of time and money, as well as kept her focused on revenue-generating business priorities.

People often ask how to tell if ideas are from their mind or their intuition. One way to tell is that intuition comes quickly. You don't have to analyze things to receive intuitive insights. How you feel about the information is also an indicator. Feeling enthusiastic and energized is a sign it is your intuition. Feeling bored, drained or anxious is a sign that it coming from your mind.

Using Intuition to Select the Best Support and Partners

If you regularly check in for intuitive support when you need to hire a virtual assistant, technical support staff, web site designer and so on, your intuition will help you determine the best fit for collaboration and referral partners. You still need to check background and expertise and then go with your intuition for the best fit for your business needs.

When her administrative assistant quit, Amanda needed to replace her quickly. She came to me with a list of eight applicants she had identified. Based on a description of the position she wanted to fill and only the first names of the applicants, I tuned in intuitively to each of the names in turn and determined their background, expertise, work ethic, personality type and who was the best fit for the job. We narrowed it down to the top two candidates who would be good fits for Amanda. She tells people how spending one hour together saved her $3,000 in the time she would have spent interviewing all eight applicants. This was time she freed for billable work. Amanda and her new administrative assistant are both thrilled with the fit.

Intuitive Tips for Powerful Results

Remember that information and answers are around you all the time. Pay closer attention to notice and understand the messages. Spend a few minutes a day asking questions that will reveal the answers you are looking for and remember to wait for the answers in all forms in which they come.

What are you seeing with your inner eyes? What are you hearing with your inner ears? What are you feeling in your body? What are you "just knowing"? These are all intuitive ways to receive insights and answers.

- **Focus.** When expanding your ability to consciously engage your intuition in business, it helps to be quiet and uninterrupted, so you can focus. Relax, take a few deep breaths, close your eyes, release all distractions and center your attention on your question or topic.

- **Ask.** Be clear about what you are asking and state it in the positive. Ask questions that will allow you to gain practical insights that are actionable in business. Some examples include: What am I to know that will help me with ___ (fill in the blank)? What is holding my business/project back and how can I resolve it? What do my prospects/clients want from me? What is the best approach for ___? What is my greatest revenue-producing opportunity?
- **Pay Attention.** Wait for the answer! And remember that it comes in various forms using the six intuitive senses.
- **Act.** Take action on the intuitive answers you receive. When you acknowledge, validate and act on your intuition, it expands.

Your intuition is like a muscle—the more you exercise it, the stronger it becomes. Besides intentionally taking a few minutes a day for this intuitive query process, there are other times when you are naturally more relaxed and where it is easier to notice answers.

One is in the fully relaxed state between sleep and opening your eyes. When you first awaken, take a moment before you jump out of bed, keep your eyes closed and notice what you notice.

Your dreams are also a great way to receive insights and answers.

Any activity associated with water, such as showering, bathing, being around water and drinking it, helps heighten your intuition. Consider keeping a notebook next to your bed or in the bathroom to record your intuitive insights while they are fresh.

Intuitions also often come while driving, so consider keeping a small digital recorder in your glove compartment for easily and safely capturing them.

It may be easier when you are learning to engage your intuition to experiment or work with a friend, colleague or professional intuitive. It can help to get intuitive insights from someone who is not attached to the outcome and who can help you see the forest and the trees. When working with someone, keep your eyes closed or averted since eye contact engages the left-brain thinking mind and can draw you away from your right-brain intuition. Be sure to agree to confidentiality with your partner.

"Your time is limited, so don't waste it living someone else's life. Don't be trapped by dogma—which is living with the results of other people's thinking. Don't let the noise of other's opinions drown out your own inner voice. And most important, have the courage to follow your heart and intuition. They somehow already know what you truly want to become. Everything else is secondary."
—Steve Jobs, American inventor and entrepreneur, co-founder of Apple Inc.®

Consider keeping an intuition journal to keep track of when you use your intuition to benefit your business. By tapping into your intuition, you will gain clarity, confidence and courage. Your business already knows what it truly wants to become. Learn to tune in with your intuition and let it tell you, so you can be clear and take focused action with what you discover.

Susan Rueppel, PhD

Founder, Owner, Business Intuitive
Chief Intuition Officer™
Immediate Answers for
Tangible Re$ults in Business
(916) 444-1112
susan@chiefintuitionofficer.com
www.chiefintuitionofficer.com

Susan Rueppel, PhD, is an internationally known business intuition expert, speaker, author and trainer. Her gift is her ability to artfully blend over fifteen years as a professional intuitive with her business acumen from twenty-plus years in corporate America designing and implementing information technology solutions. As a business intuitive, she works with entrepreneurs, business owners and corporate professionals who desire to create or grow their businesses quicker and easier. Her clients call her a "combination intuitive search engine and GPS," providing immediate answers and a roadmap with a clearer vision, specific strategies and prioritized path forward. In her consultations, training and mentoring with thousands of clients, she makes intuition practical and accessible in all areas of business, wellness and balance.

Whether speaking on intuition in business or intuition in sales, Susan's lively and engaging presentation style inspires people to recognize and illuminate their personal and professional genius.

Susan's vision is to help generate a soul-based business revolution by inspiring entrepreneurial professionals to use intuition as a valuable business resource in order to serve more people doing what they love and creating an abundant income. Susan lives in the Sacramento, California, area.

■ ■ ■

Cast Aside Business Building Busters to Ensure Your Success

By Caterina Rando, MA, MCC

You know you need marketing skills, you know you need sales skills, you know you need to provide excellent customer care to make your business profitable and sustainable. That is just the beginning. To be a truly extraordinary entrepreneur who continues to grow your business, it is also important to look at how you behave at the helm of your company.

This chapter covers some of the biggest business growth busters I have seen over and over that prevent entrepreneurs from accelerating the growth of their businesses. I include them in this book for you because my experience as a twenty-year business coach and strategist has shown me that most of the time, the offending entrepreneur is not even aware of what they are doing that is holding them back. Read these pages and see if you recognize yourself in any of the business busters discussed.

1. Waiting for Ready

I have a talented, gifted, gracious, smart client who is frequently waiting until everything is totally figured out—a course must be 100 percent written before it is marketed, or every last tweak of a website is necessary before it goes live, and she must have 100 percent enrollment in a group before she launches an event. Because of this consistent behavior, it takes her forever to do anything, and her business is not growing. Does any of this ring a bell for you?

Instead of waiting for ready, do the opposite and be willing to create and learn as you go. Maybe that sounds scary, and I will not deny that it is. However, learning and creating as you go keeps you in forward motion. Waiting for ready is staying in the same place and being stagnant while you get everything completed.

Let's be very clear: A successful business is in a constant state of stretching, reinventing and adjusting. You, as the entrepreneur, are best served by also being in a constant state of stretching, reinventing, adjusting and learning.

Ask yourself right now: In what areas are you waiting for ready and what is that costing you? Next question: What are you going to do about it?

Be willing to be uncomfortable while you are creating, learning and growing. This is your key to running a truly extraordinary business.

2. Over Planning and Overlearning

Many times, an entrepreneur will tell me they are planning a project, and when I talk to them the next month, they are still planning the same project. It is not that they did not have time for the planning—they have been doing the planning and doing the planning and doing the planning. In other words, they have been over planning. Get in action already!

Another thing related to this is overlearning. This happens when entrepreneurs attend a different workshop or seminar several times a month. Do not get me wrong, I am all for personal and professional development. However, many entrepreneurs spend so much time attending programs that they keep looking *outside* themselves for answers, rather than applying what they have already learned and increasing their real business experience.

Sometimes, I have had to say to coaching clients, "Get out of the workshops and get to work!"

Over planning and overlearning often comes from not trusting yourself and your skills enough, and not trusting your ability to be flexible and work out any challenges that come up.

Take a deep breath and ask yourself if there are any areas where you are over planning. The solution is to give yourself a deadline and stick to it to prove to yourself that you do not have to have every aspect or everything figured out before you get going. This will build your confidence and make it so that you will plan less and act more.

3. Saying Yes When You Want to Say No

I want you to say "yes" often in your business. A "yes" gives you new opportunities, builds relationships and creates clients. Sometimes, we say "yes" when we really want to say "no."

Recently I spent the day speaking at a conference that I should not have been speaking at. Not because the audience was not the right match, or I needed to be somewhere else. I should not have been there because it was the first time this conference was held, and I know that the first year a conference is held they rarely get the numbers they project. Because of saying "yes" when I wanted to say "no," I gave a keynote speech to a 95-percent-empty ballroom. For the first time in twenty years, no one attended my breakout session.

Why do you say "yes" when you want to say "no"?

We want to be nice or supportive or do not want to disappoint anyone. The truth is, our experience or perspective often knows better!

You have to put yourself and your business first, ahead of other people's priorities. One thing I have learned is that when you say "no," someone might be disappointed for about two minutes until they think of whom to ask next to chair the benefit or run the meeting or pick someone up at the airport.

Say "no" when you want to. This is a lesson you may have to learn over and over. I know I do. Is there any area of your life where you said "yes" when you really wanted to say "no"? If so, go say "no" now!

4. Not Making Decisions Quickly

Each day in your business, you have many decisions to make. Too many entrepreneurs take too long to make decisions. This slows down the rate at which business is conducted.

Most decisions are not business threatening. They are as innocuous as selecting Italian or Mexican food for lunch or picking up roses or spring flowers for the office. Still, so many entrepreneurs are afraid of making any missteps or spending even a little money that they take forever to make the smallest decisions.

Don't let this be you. Instead, consider the worst thing that can happen. Sometimes you waste some money or on the upside, that sales or marketing person you are considering hiring could catapult your business. Be willing to try new things for your business and spend some money here and there to see what works and does not. Do not spend hours on research, do not ask the opinion of several people and do not endlessly check references.

Successful people make decisions quickly. Put attention on accelerating your decision-making skills. Where is your business right now? Have you been slow to make a decision? Make that decision right now.

5. Having to Have It All Figured Out Before You Act

There is a lot to be said for making it up as you go along. Let's say you are hosting a public workshop to gain new clients in four weeks. Do you have to have your entire curriculum finalized and the handouts designed before you start to fill the event? If you think so, then this buster is for you.

Often, I talk to people who are working on a project like a tele-summit, a seminar, a new product or a new service and they keep it under wraps until it is 100 percent done. Here is what happens when this is the procedure you follow: It takes two to six times as long as anticipated or planned for to complete the project. This slows down your business and your revenue growth.

Instead, announce something before it is done. The launch date serves as your deadline and cannot be missed. This causes creativity, momentum and, best of all, urgency in your business. Creating urgency in your business is a huge skill to embrace to accelerate your productivity. This also creates revenue growth. Ask yourself right now: Where would it serve you in your business today to act before you have it all figured out?

6. Need to Get It Right the First Time

When you have a need to get it right the first time, you might write and rewrite a newsletter over and over, or you might keep redesigning and reworking your website and not launch it for months. You keep giving away your services free of charge because you do not think you are quite good enough yet to start charging.

You might record a video for your website and never post it because it is not exactly the way you want it. You might host a webinar or special event for your clients, and it might not go well. You might lose money the first time and decide never to do it again, to the detriment of your business.

I tell my business coaching clients that they cannot actually determine if a specific marketing or revenue-producing strategy is viable until they have done it three times. This gives you the experience of the first time, followed by the upgrades of the second time and, combined with the buzz that is now in place for the third time, you achieve success.

Where in your business would it serve you to not be attached to getting it right the first time?

7. Doing It All Yourself

This success buster will keep your business small and very unstable because you are doing activities that are not revenue producing, are less focused on adding new clients and are not taking care of the clients you already have.

Think about rock stars. Their job is to master their performance and create new music. They have people who handle everything else. They do not sew costumes, design ads or answer the phone when someone wants to know where they will be performing. Just like a rock star, your job is to perform and master your talent and do the things that only you can do. To succeed, focus your energy and time on what you do best. Have a team to help you with everything else.

What is your talent? What are the things that only you can do? If you are a graphic designer, only you can design your clients' logos. If you are a writer, only you can put words on paper. If you are a trainer, only you can get on the stage and deliver your program. These are your revenue-producing activities, and this is where you want to put your focus. The people on your team support you by creating systems, serving clients, processing data and doing what you need done. This lets you focus on what you do best so you move toward success. Your support team helps you achieve your business objectives. Any time you perform an activity that is not the highest and best use of your professional time, you hold back your business. See "Hiring the Right People" by Cynthia Fassler on page 217.

What are you doing that is not the highest and best use of your time? Are you bookkeeping, updating your website, designing marketing emails and newsletters? What are you doing that someone else can do? Get the support you need and watch your business grow.

8. Believing in the Myth of Right Timing

Often I see entrepreneurs say "no" to new opportunities because they think they are not ready yet, the opportunity is coming at a time when they have other things going on, or they are not sure if they can handle it. Being successful in business requires being willing to be uncomfortable. In fact, being willing to be uncomfortable is a skill that will accelerate your business.

Life rarely delivers what you want in the perfect time. There is no right time for a "yes" for the next best thing in your business. When opportunities present themselves, say "yes" and then figure out how to make it work.

Where in your business is it time to let go of the myth of right timing?

9. Turning Green with Envy

It makes me sad when entrepreneurs talk about what everyone else is doing and how depressed or debilitated they feel because they are not doing the same thing.

I always encourage my clients to take their attention off their colleagues or competitors and keep their attention on what they want to achieve with their business and how to get there. When you see someone who has achieved tremendous success, be happy for them and let their success serve as an affirmation that your next success breakthrough is on its way.

Congratulate others for their success and be genuinely interested in hearing all about it. Celebrate the success of others, and you will enjoy celebrating your successes more as well. Envy is like worry—it is a wasted emotion that does not serve you or your business. Keep your eye on your next target, not on other people, or you will not notice your ship, your big break or your next revenue stream when it does come in.

Look at this list of business building busters and pick the ones that you think are affecting you. Keep these in mind as you continue with your business and do your best to continue to bust through them. When you do, your business will grow and flourish, and I promise you will amaze yourself.

Caterina Rando, MA, MCC

Business Strategist, Speaker, Publisher

Making you and your business Thrive

(415) 668-4535

cat@caterinarando.com

www.caterinarando.com

www.caterinaspeaks.com

www.thrivebooks.com

Caterina Rando's mission is to show entrepreneurs how to be loud and proud about who they are and the value they bring. She is a sought-after speaker, business strategist and author of the national bestseller, *Learn to Power Think* from Chronicle Books. She is featured as a success expert in several leading business books including *Build It Big, Get Clients Now, Get Slightly Famous, Incredible Business* and *Make Your Connections Count.*

Since 1993, Caterina has been providing consulting, training and solutions to ensure entrepreneurs succeed. Through her Business Breakthrough Summit, Sought After Speaker Summit and Luxury Retreat for Women Entrepreneurs, she and her team show entrepreneurs how to become recognized as experts, think and plan strategically and significantly grow their revenue.

Caterina is also the founder of THRIVE Publishing™, a company that publishes multi-author books, including this book, for experts who want to share their message with a greater market. She holds a bachelor of science degree in organizational behavior and a master of arts degree in life transitions counseling psychology. She is a certified personal and professional coach (CPPC) and a master certified coach (MCC), the highest designation awarded by the International Coaching Federation™.

■ ■ ■

Overcoming Fear to Seize Opportunities

By LeTonya F. Moore, Esq.

Are you the person who wishes they could do big wonderful and grandiose things? Have you longed to make a career change or move in another direction? Have you taken an inventory and found several missed chances for success? Do you want to own your own business, yet you do not think you have what it takes? In life, opportunities are all around. Some are blatantly obvious, while others are latent. What happens when an opportunity is presented? Many people create ways and reasons they should not take it. The billion-dollar question is, why? Why are we afraid to seize the moment? What prevents us from recognizing the big break? How do we sever the ties that bind?

To become fully cognizant of where you want and need to be, you must first examine your present situation. Typically, we build our lives so that we are content in our "comfort zone." The comfort zone represents what is stable, familiar or non-threatening to the status quo. It is a direct result of insecurities that have manifested due to internal and external factors. These factors create our unwillingness to stretch beyond our limits, color outside the lines and cross through the barriers. This has created a culture of fear that presents insurmountable obstacles for many. To overcome this fear, you must use obstacles as stepping-stones. You must free your mind to view your circumstance from the right perspective and use these experiences to grow.

Where Are You?

Ask yourself a very serious question, "Is my outlook affecting my outcome?"

What we are taught through our nurturing, what we see in society and how we view ourselves within societal norms culminate in our outlook. Our trepidation with seeking and seizing opportunities is related to limitations placed upon us, our self-view and others' views. To figure out where you are, perform a self-assessment by answering the following:

1. Describe your ultimate goal for your future.
2. What are key obstacles in accomplishing your ultimate goal?
3. What are some short-term goals for the next three-, six- and nine-month periods to help you move toward the ultimate goal?
4. What support do you need to achieve these goals? How can you obtain the support that you need in this area?
5. In what areas would you like to grow and develop? What are your strategies for this growth and development?

Alberto, a long-term client, is a very proud man. For most of his life, he dreamed of owning his own restaurant to better support his family. At this time, Alberto was in his forties and had a great job working for a local manufacturing company. When he completed his self-assessment, it confirmed that he wanted to own a restaurant. His barriers consisted of lack of capital, education and knowledge of the restaurant business. It also revealed that he had not undertaken any self-help remedies to address his barriers. He was able to set some short-and long-term goals for reaching his dream.

After you complete your self-assessment, review your answers regarding obstacles to accomplishing your ultimate goal. When you look beneath the surface, how many of your answers come from a fear of going for your goal? To conquer and overcome fear, you must identify the root cause.

"Go confidently in the direction of your dreams. Live the life you have imagined."
—Henry David Thoreau, American author and poet

Success Key #1: Before you know where you are going, you have to know where you are.

What Is the Root Cause?

In seeking the root cause for your fears, the goal is to identify problems or events that are the true reasons you shy away from challenges. By conducting a root cause analysis, you can determine the core of your fear.

The development of a mindset is essentially like planting a tree. You start with planting a seed, which is the initial act or event. The root-cause revelation is the seed that took root within your mind. This has created a belief system by which you assess opportunities.

Your conditioning comes from the nurturing that you received throughout your development. How was your seed watered? Once your sprout began to grow, were you protected from weeds? Did you receive the right amount of sunlight to flourish? Approaching opportunities with a fearful mind has a direct correlation with your conditioning. The resulting fruit is your life perspective.

Start with your present situation and think about the shortcomings that you identified in your self-assessment. Take the following steps:

- Work backwards from each identified shortcoming and determine the earliest point in time you were cognizant of it. What was happening at this point in your life?
- For each point, identify the factors and causes of this.
- Classify causes into those of which you were in control and those of which you were not in control.
- Identify actions that you could have taken that would prevent recurrence of each harmful effect and include outcomes and factors.
- Set goals to implement each action and develop an action plan.
- Implement your action plan.

When evaluating the deep seeds of his hesitancy to start his business, Alberto conducted his root-causes analysis. In working through the first three steps, he realized he had feelings of inferiority that were directly related to his failure to complete his education. He disclosed that many days his father would take him out of school to earn money for the family. This made him fall behind in his courses, and, eventually, he never returned to school.

Alberto came to the realization that this was beyond his control. He acknowledged that as a child he was bound to what his parents needed from him.

In working through the remaining steps, Alberto came to appreciate his present situation and created a plan to compensate for his lack of education. He recognized that despite no formal education, he had accomplished many things in his life. He started to study restaurateurs Ray Kroc, creative genius behind McDonald's Hamburgers® and Dave Thomas, founder of Wendy's Hamburgers®. Both men came from humble beginnings. This helped Alberto view his situation in a different way.

Success Key #2: Whatever you let take root will grow.

What Is Your Perspective?

Alberto initially allowed his view of being uneducated and illiterate to overshadow his skills. After discovering Ray Kroc and Dave Thomas, he realized that they were no different from him. He knew he had several options of which he could take advantage and made up his mind to take control of his destiny.

"When you have options, anything is bearable. It's when a situation is inescapable that it becomes hell."
—Michelle Williams, American actress, Academy Award® nominee

The way you deal with opportunities is all about perspective. When you are looking from the perspective that a situation is inescapable, then it is.

I challenge you to believe you always have options! Are you willing to examine and change your perspective? In addressing the question, "How do you overcome your fears to seize opportunities?" you must change your perspective, acknowledge your shortcomings and understand your culture of fear. Life's weeds are our shortcomings. But, everyone has them. You cannot allow the preverbal weed to choke the life from your dreams.

Success Key #3: If someone else has already achieved it, so can you.

The Culture of Fear

Fears are a result of years of conditioning and forced conformity, and they manifest in your outcomes. Many people spend valuable time focusing on past misdeeds or events, and they are controlled by their past and the negative consequences of ill-considered decisions. Others are haunted by the "sins of the father" and are crippled by the disgrace of their lineage.

When our coaching relationship started, Alberto talked about the business venture he had always wanted to do as a child. He discussed how he would tell his parents and older relatives about it, and they would tell him that it would never happen for him. While working through the coaching process, Alberto revealed that he could not read very well. He disclosed that every time he tried to improve, it would not work. His homework was to locate adult literacy courses in the local area and make a commitment to enroll. Alberto never enrolled in the course. He admitted that he felt he had been out of school for more than twenty years and was ashamed and afraid to enroll for fear of "looking dumb or stupid." He allowed the culture of fear to prevent him from moving toward his ultimate goal.

Fears are fortified by what you think, say and do. Your experiences shape you into the person you have become. When you live in the culture of fear, you lack the ability to see your true value and potential. Have you ever thought: "I'm not good enough," "I'm not important enough," or "I'm not smart enough"?

Have you ever discovered an advancement opportunity for which you were qualified and decided not to apply because someone else applied? Do you fade into the woodwork during a presentation for upper management?

Do you focus on your weaknesses because you were taught not to "brag" about yourself? Just like Alberto, have you allowed fear to control your mind, words and deeds?

"You don't have to think a thought just because it comes into your head!"
—Joyce Meyer, American evangelist

When you have thoughts, speak words and perform actions that cultivate fear, you produce a negative self-view and create insecurities about your abilities.

When the people who are the closest to you speak negativity, and you allow these words to take hold, they become a self-fulfilling prophecy. This is what Alberto had done. There are many reasons why families make these statements. However, at some point in your life, you have to realize you are in control of your outcomes.

Success Key #4: If your thoughts, words or actions are negative, the result is negative.

When you become aware of why you have a certain outlook, you can start to reposition your focus from where you are and why you are there to where you want to be.

"Nothing can stop the man with the right mental attitude from achieving his goal, nothing on Earth can help the man with the wrong mental attitude."
—Thomas Jefferson, third president of the United States

You are well on your way to the ultimate destination! You have analyzed your current situation, uncovered the root cause of your fearfulness and examined your level of control over these factors. By working the implementation plan you developed as part of your self-assessment, you can move forward toward your ultimate destination. Be confident and self-assured.

Create the Culture of Confidence

Having a sense of confidence is a life skill. As with any other skill, it is a learned behavior and gets better the more you practice. An effective way to improve your self-confidence is to create a confidence toolkit. Your toolkit should consist of the ability to dig deep within yourself, the wherewithal to withstand trials, the desire to succeed, the humility to accept compliments with grace and courage to overcome any obstacle.

Use these tools to change your views about your abilities. Believe you are worthy of obtaining your desired reality and replace negative thoughts with positive thoughts. Above all else, accept yourself as you are in this moment. You may not have all that you need to reach your destination right now—you will! Reposition your destructive thoughts and view obstacles as steps, not barriers, to success.

Changing your views also means being mindful of what you say and how you say it. When taking an inventory of what you need to do to get to your final destination, speak about it in a "half-full" rather than a "half-empty" way. Your words are a manifestation of your thoughts. Change your thoughts, and you will change your words. Now that you have repositioned your thinking, changed your words and adjusted your deeds, you are ready to build your legacy.

What is Your Legacy?

Our legacy is the story of our lives. Both the self-assessment and the root-cause analysis you have conducted, are an examination of what your legacy would look like at this moment. This is not the end. You can redirect your passion and become a conqueror. What do you think your legacy would be? How would those who know you best describe you?

Now that you know who, what, when and from where your dream limitations have evolved, you can get motivated to build your legacy. Each time a destructive thought enters your mind, refocus on the toolkit you created. If portions of your self-assessment identified skills that need enhancement, make a decision to sharpen those skills. Highlight your strengths without arrogance and compensate for any drawbacks. These are seeds of change for you. External factors, once mastered, will help you stay confident in seizing opportunities.

To remain on the path to success, know your friends and foes. Your friends are the people who are beneficial to your journey. They are those who are willing to encourage and uplift you. They may not be the people with which you have personal and social relationships, and they are invested in your success. Your foes are people who, even with good intentions, reinforce your culture of fear. They are the people who try to force you to focus on "What if it does not work out?" and "What is your plan B?"

"Every great dream begins with a dreamer. Always remember, you have within you the strength, the patience, and the passion to reach for the stars to change the world."
—Harriet Tubman, African-America former slave, abolitionist and humanitarian

Success Key #5: Remain faithful in your abilities and hopeful for the future.

Overcome Fears and Seize Opportunities!

Seizing opportunities without fear can be achieved by following the five basic steps to properly prepare for success. The five steps are:

1. Take the self-assessment.
2. Determine the root cause of fear.
3. Acknowledge and address your culture of fear.
4. Prepare your culture of confidence toolkit.
5. Follow the winning formula:

Meditation + Affirmation + Verbalization = Realization.

By following this formula for three months, these tools will become habits. Are you willing to invest three months in yourself? For thirty days, take seven to ten minutes per day to meditate on the quotes and success keys in this chapter. Allow them to become part of your belief system with regard to how you view your opportunities.

During days thirty-one to sixty, print out each key and quote and display them in areas you frequent throughout your day. When one of them draws your attention, take some time to read it.

From days sixty-one to ninety, identify the keys and quotes that are most applicable to your situation. Take seven to ten minutes a day and read each one aloud. Substitute your name or use "I" in the appropriate places. When you personalize these statements, they will become your realization.

LeTonya F. Moore, Esq.

CEO, Opulence Enterprises, LLC

"M.O.V.E. Beyond Limits!"

(256) 434-1605
www.oppcoach.com
letonya.faye@oppcoach.com

LeTonya is "The Opportunity Coach"! She developed the M.O.V.E. concept to **M**otivate clients to find and seize **O**pportunities, to lead them to **V**ictory, through active engagement and **E**xecuting action plans! She teaches that your perspective is your reality—that your thoughts, words and actions are a direct correlation with what happens in your life. She shows you how to change your perspective to change your reality!

LeTonya provides her clients with tools necessary to change their outlook and produce a positive outcome. Through her M.O.V.E. program, she provides post-program support to ensure continued success. Her passion is to utilize her expertise to improve the lives of others through coaching and providing quality legal services to the underserved. Her coaching practice targets four specific groups—entrepreneurs, trial litigation, performance improvement and career development.

As a licensed attorney, LeTonya combines her legal expertise and coaching skills to build both advisory and substantive client relationships. She has developed several seminars and training modules tailored for entrepreneurs at every level. Her presentations are entertaining, informative and inspiring. LeTonya has a national client base. Her business, Opulence Enterprises, is located in Tampa, FL.

■ ■ ■

Mind Your Mind

To Grow Your Business

By Brenda Lee Gallatin, MA ABS, CDC, CLC, CDV

Business is challenging, sometimes overwhelming and sometimes downright tough. All of this can make you, as an entrepreneur, sometimes feel like you just do not have what it takes to be successful. Here is what I want you to know: you can be anything you want to be, if only you believe with sufficient conviction and act in accordance with your beliefs.

"Whatever the mind can conceive and believe, the mind can achieve."
–Napoleon Hill, American author

To be a successful entrepreneur, it is imperative to make sure that there is no "stinkin' thinkin'" in your business.

What about when you don't feel extraordinary, invincible or that you can keep going? That is what we are going to discuss in this chapter. The more attention you put on believing in yourself, the more successful your business will be.

Your mind is the greatest power tool you have—it is the source of all your creation. Therefore, wouldn't it be prudent to learn more about it and pay more attention to it and all its marvelous capabilities? Wouldn't it be beneficial to guard your mind, your thoughts and what you fill it with? So much attention is put on looking successful and not enough on what is essentially our personal command center. Your mind is involved in and is controlling absolutely everything you do, including how you think, feel and act.

In an article written by Khan Sajid on November 16, 2011, he offered an interesting metaphor for the brain/mind when he said, "The brain is the engine, while the car is the physical body of the human being, where the mind is the driver of this car of life." With that in mind, we could say that your thoughts are the fuel for the car that gets you everywhere you want to go in life.

You may have heard it said that you become what you think about, or—put another way—what you think about comes about, and what you think about expands. I believe that you get where you want to be or not by the thoughts that you think and that your thoughts are so powerful that they determine your destiny.

We entrepreneurs are generally positive and upbeat, enthusiastic and unstoppable, adventurous risk takers. I rarely hear anyone talk about the inner struggles of being an entrepreneur and even more rarely do I hear successful entrepreneurs talk about when they are not feeling so extraordinary.

Many factors play into our psyche and contribute to how we feel, how we function in the world and who we become. I grew up in a shame-based atmosphere that has taken a lifetime and lots of hard knocks to turn around. I took on some Life Commandments that were embedded deep in my soul.

When I was a youngster growing up in a small conservative town in New England, my family was shattered and broken. It was a crazy atmosphere. Fun and love blended with alcoholism, physical and emotional abuse. Our home was filled with broken furniture, broken hearts and broken promises. At age five, I watched my dad being taken away by the police after an intense physical fight with my mom. I was terrified and screaming as our neighbor took my sister and me to the safety of their home. Yet another layer of shame and embarrassment was added when I wet my pants and peed on their floor—the neighbor was so angry and scolding and shaming. No one that age wets their pants.

Where I grew up way back in the 40s and 50s, divorce was a disgrace and alcoholism and violence were kept very secret. When my parents were divorced, mom was excommunicated from the church and, suddenly, none of my playmates were allowed to come to my home. Shame was being heaped on us, but how were any of us to know about the impact of such things before the days of workshops, counseling and so on? Being a single mom raising two daughters was no small task and from then on, my mom worked every day and most evenings to keep food on the table and keep us together. Consequently, I was alone most of the time. I became very independent, rebellious and unruly, and acted out in unacceptable behaviors. I was often sent to the principal's office and expelled from time to time. At school, I was singled out as that girl from a bad home. I ran with a rough crowd and got into plenty of trouble. It was very hard on my mother. You might imagine the toll it took on my *self-esteem*.

However, the little girl on the inside of that tough exterior who was crying for love and attention in all the wrong ways had several things going for her. The fun-loving girl was an extrovert, leader, caring, generous, friendly, smart, talented and responsible. I was an excellent little sales lady—in my first experience in sales, I sold the most Girl

Scout cookies. I loved to sing and tap dance and was always chosen to be on stage. I loved performing in plays and entertaining people and got a lot of positive attention for my talents.

I met my husband on a blind date when I was fourteen and he was in the Navy stationed in Boston. I dropped out of school in the fall of my junior year and married at age sixteen. The word around town was we wouldn't last a year. Five decades later, here we are—two happy lovers. By age twenty-five, I had five children and had another six years later. We have five sons and one daughter. What I want to convey to you is that for some of us entrepreneurs, it is a journey of ups and downs, starts and stops. It is not always all positive and fun because of our earliest years and the Unconscious Life Commandments we internalized. These commandments can continue to show up as *"stinkin' thinkin'"* and plague us without warning for a lifetime. It takes intentional effort to become aware of your negative Life Commandments and to break them.

Here is how Unconscious Life Commandments are affecting your mind and everyday life.

- Unconscious Life Commandments are internal rules we live by. Life commandments can be kinesthetically inferred and most are instilled in the first couple of years of a child's life.
- Unconscious Life Commandments are transitory. They work at one time, and then they become dysfunctional later. Life Commandments can change.
- Unconscious Life Commandments are locked in at around 8-9 years of age. These are vulnerable years for a child. It's the age at which a child begins to believe the Life Commandments that they have been given.

- An Unconscious Life Commandment is our inner guidance system. Life Commandments are the gyros of the *mind*. They are the automatic pilot of our behavior system.
- You have both negative and positive Life Commandments.
- We need to learn to be "disobedient" to some of our Unconscious Life Commandments. We need to learn how to break the ones that are not serving us today.

Unconscious Life Commandments Instilled in Early Childhood That Are Not Serving You

1. Children should be seen and not heard.

If you internalize this as truth, it may impact you by closing off your ability to speak up and share your feelings and ideas—you believe you do not matter, you must keep quiet, you are a bother and what you have to say does not matter. If this sounds like what you heard growing up, it is time to remind yourself that what you have to say has value and to make a choice to speak your mind and share your ideas.

2. You will never be good enough.

Believing this negative Life Commandment robs you of confidence and is exhausting. You are always striving to do and be good enough while never feeling like you are. This belief manifests as approval seeking, depression, procrastination, and you may unconsciously have a tendency to sabotage your success. If this sounds like you, it is time for you to know that you *are* good enough, you *do* have value to bring and it *is* time to start to bring it.

3. We cannot afford it.

Hearing this while growing up implants scarcity thinking in your mind, fear and embarrassment and a belief that you are unworthy, resulting in a lifetime of money problems. You may be indecisive and second-guess yourself on many levels, causing you to miss opportunities for joy, freedom and prosperity. If you find this idea resonating with you, it is time to take on your finances, increase your income and become more confident about your spending. It does take money to make money.

4. Keep your thoughts to yourself.

If you heard this a lot growing up, you believe no one wants to hear what you think because whatever it is, it is not important. You hesitate to speak up, then someone else expresses the thought or answer you have on the tip of your tongue and you feel invisible. You live on the periphery, always holding back and not fully committed and engaged in moving your life and business forward. If this early life idea is in your way, it is time to embrace sharing your thoughts—maybe even time to take a public speaking class or teach a class. Do things to reinforce that your thoughts have merit.

5. You really do not feel that way.

This is set up early in life when you express tears or frustration and you are told, "*Stop it* or I will give you something to be upset about." It's as if someone outside of you is deciding what you are feeling. You lack confidence and doubt yourself. You feel confused and lack conviction for your ideas, your products, your business. If this seems like something that may be going on for you, it is time to start paying more attention to your feelings, developing your intuition and trusting how you feel. Become more aware of your feelings and remember that all feelings are valid and neither good nor bad.

6. Let me do it for you, I will take care of it.

This is a perfect setup for feeling incompetent and afraid to make mistakes. You learn to rely on others and you hold back and wait for someone else to step up and do it because you lack the confidence to do it right. You miss the opportunity to take risks and try new things. If this sounds like you, it is time to start to take a risk every day—big risks and small risks. With each uncomfortable thing you do, you remind yourself that you can handle whatever business or life requires of you.

7. Life is not fair.

If this is one of your Unconscious Life Commandments, you may walk around with a chip on your shoulder and believe that the world owes you and that everyone is out to get you. When anything goes wrong for you, it is not your fault. Your attitude comes across as arrogant and haughty and drives prospective friends and business away from you. If you are living with this, you are one of those people that other people do not much like to be around. Knock that chip off your shoulder and recognize that life is what you make it. It is time to start applying yourself to improve yourself to be the best you can be.

8. You are so stupid.

Unfortunately, this Unconscious Life Commandment can make you feel defeated even before you get going. You can feel you are not smart enough to accomplish anything worthwhile. It is a debilitating idea that will hold you back from pursuing your dreams.

This one can often go undetected and cause you to not stretch yourself and try new things. If you ever find yourself telling yourself you are "so stupid," that will be an obvious sign that this idea is under your skin and impacting your behavior.

This one is combated mostly by paying attention to how you speak and think about yourself.

9. Why can't you be as good as your sister/brother, ______________?

You are set up to believe you are a disappointment and will never measure up to the expectations of others. Although you have desires, great intentions and put forth effort, you sabotage yourself. While comparisons are necessary in life, they can be very traumatic for children. If you find yourself feeling or thinking that you are not as good as others, remind yourself that you are capable and competent and what others are doing does not matter.

10. Do not talk back.

This is another paralyzing Unconscious Life Commandment that inhibits you from speaking up, expressing yourself and asking for what you want. Because you heard this message a lot while growing up, you are often afraid to make suggestions and present ideas, to address objections and close the sale. When clients identify that this is a message they heard too often and it is affecting them today, I encourage them to set a goal to at least once a day every day, have a conversation that makes them uncomfortable.

Take a few moments and identify the Unconscious Life Commandments that you heard growing up and might be impacting your life. Go ahead and make a list. Once you have completed your list and identified your Unconscious Life Commandments, you can then become conscious of them and begin to break those commandments.

In addition to the ideas discussed, consider writing a letter to whomever you want to in order to break an Unconscious Life Commandment. You do not send this letter. You can write it whether the person is alive or already passed. Here is a list of things to include:

- State that you are breaking an Unconscious Life Commandment.
- State that you have self-respect, honor and dignity.
- Explain how it was for you and how it felt when you heard this Unconscious Life Commandment.
- Describe what you think this Unconscious Life Commandment has cost you.

- State that you are reclaiming your self-worth.
- State that you reject this Unconscious Life Commandment.
- Forgive the offender.

This can be a very liberating and empowering experience if you choose to do the work.

As an entrepreneur on the path to being extraordinary, you have a mission in life that is worth working for. Some of that work must be done from the inside out. When you truly and unapologetically believe in yourself, speak your mind and share your gifts, nothing can stop you from achieving success. Mind your mind and watch your success soar.

Brenda Lee Gallatin, MA ABS, CDC, CLC, CDV

Anything is possible if you believe in yourself and mind your mind

(206) 769-1700
imakelifebetter@yahoo.com
www.coach4successnow.com

Brenda Lee is an inspiring, compassionate, energetic, spunky coach. She is a seasoned professional counselor to a diverse range of people. She is also a Certified Dream Coach and a Leadership Coach. Her education, life and business experience along with her faith make her uniquely equipped to help you with discovering your life purpose and limiting beliefs and support you on your way to making your dreams a reality.

Alongside her counseling career, Brenda Lee's natural love of people, fun and excitement has always led her into sales and network marketing. She is a master at networking and discernment and particularly enjoys working the cold market. Brenda Lee has risen to the top levels, earning the number one spot for recruiting and sales. She has grown and nurtured teams, earned cars, trips and awards for her efforts. "I love network marketing," she says, and loves helping others be successful and reach their dreams and goals.

Brenda Lee wants you to believe anything is possible if you believe. On her 60th birthday, she completed the Danskin Triathlon participating as a cancer survivor.

■ ■ ■

Optimal Health for Entrepreneurs

By Tamara Cameron, HHC, AADP

As entrepreneurs, we spend a lot of time making sure that our businesses are doing well. We work long hours, research, network and upgrade our training. There is another aspect of our business that is just as important as our latest marketing, which gets less attention—our health!

We are our businesses. If we are healthy, happy and driven, our businesses will be healthy, happy and flourishing. A high level of health is a real business asset that you cannot ignore if you want big success. Here are my best tips for making easy changes to dramatically increase your health, so both you and your business thrive!

Step off the caffeine and sugar rollercoaster! A cup of coffee for breakfast, a muffin as a late-morning snack, a second cup of coffee, soda or a chocolate bar in the afternoon and wine or a cocktail after dinner as a reward for making it through another stressful day do not serve you.

If this is your routine or close to it, your health is suffering, and you are running on external energy rather than you own internal power. Just like the battery in your laptop, which stops holding a full charge when you leave it plugged into the outlet all the time, your body becomes dependent on these external stimulants for energy.

How do you break the cycle?

- **Eat breakfast.** Breakfast really is the most important meal of the day, and it needs to be nutrient dense. Eat a two-egg veggie omelet or oatmeal with blueberries, chopped walnuts and cinnamon. Start a breakfast smoothie routine. Prepping a breakfast smoothie takes the same amount of time and effort as brewing coffee, and the results are incredible!

  A basic smoothie is one cup of almond or rice milk, a big handful of frozen berries, half a banana and one kale leaf blended. This smoothie enhances your own natural energy, which will carry you through the morning.

  Don't let this routine get boring. Change up the ingredients to keep it interesting. Try different combinations of fruit and vegetables. There are lots of different smoothie recipes out there. Experiment. Discover what tastes best and works best for you.

- **Remember to breathe.** If you are feeling stressed and out of sorts, don't reach for sugar. Stop, step away from the computer and spend two minutes taking a breath break. Sit up straight, close your eyes and breathe in through your nose. There will be a natural pause at the top of the breath. Then exhale through the nose. When we breathe, we really only have control over our exhale, so exhale completely. Inhale again. Repeat this cycle of inhaling and exhaling five times. Then open your eyes. You will feel less stressed, have better mental focus and your vision will be sharper. It's true. Try it. Another great way to lower stress and increase energy through breath is to take a walking break. When you would normally reach for that second cup of coffee, get outside and cruise around the block instead. It only takes ten minutes to re-enliven your body and get your internal energy system back on line. While you are walking, put your shoulders back, straighten your posture and walk like you have some place to be. Look around, enjoy the sights, notice new things and smile. Enjoy the break and return to your workday energized.

- **Eat a serving of protein at every meal.** Protein is an energizer and will keep you going all day. This doesn't mean meat three times a day. Other great sources of protein include spinach, kale, beans, quinoa, nuts, free-range omega-3 eggs and yogurt. If you do eat meat protein, make sure you know the source, that it's organic and free-range and that your serving is no bigger than a deck of cards.

  Protein also helps you feel satiated and helps prevent overeating. Have you had the experience of eating a large salad with all kinds of vegetables for lunch and then feeling hungry 30 minutes later? You did this great thing that you thought was so good for your health, and now you are reaching for chocolate. Next time add a serving of protein—a half-cup of beans or quinoa, sliced hard-boiled egg or chopped chicken will leave you feeling full but not stuffed and will take you through the afternoon.

- **Fish is good for you.** It provides omega-3 fatty acids, which are good for your heart and brain and help to decrease inflammation. Yet large fish, which are at the top of the fish food chain, may contain high levels of contaminants, such as heavy metals and PCBs. PCB stands for polychlorinated biphenyl, which is a persistent organic pollutant, in other words, it's toxic and it doesn't go away.

Even though PCBs were banned in the U.S. in 1979, they are still hanging around in the food chain. Because large fish eat smaller fish, the bigger the fish, the higher the concentration of these sorts of contaminants. If possible, eat the smaller fish that are at the beginning of the food chain, such as herring, sardines and mackerel. They eat mostly algae, which has little to no contamination.

Farmed fish are not the best. They have a lower concentration of omega-3, and most fish farms are crowded. Like us, fish that don't exercise aren't healthy. To keep them from getting sick, they are fed antibiotics, which stay in the meat. If you are going to eat salmon, halibut or other larger fish, stick with wild-caught and don't eat it more than once or twice a week. Vegetarian sources of omega-3 include flax seeds, which can be ground and sprinkled on most anything, walnuts and pecans.

- **Stop eating starch and processed carbs, in other words, no white food.** With the exception of cauliflower, white food is an energy sapper. It slows you down and makes you feel sluggish. Consumption of processed carbs is also linked to every major lifestyle disease including obesity, diabetes, heart disease and cancer. Switch to eating a variety of nutrient-dense vegetables, fruit and whole grains every day.

  Eat fresh foods that are all the colors of the rainbow with an emphasis on green. Each differently colored fruit and vegetable provides micronutrients that enhance your health. Two servings of cruciferous vegetables, such as kale, broccoli, Brussels sprouts, arugula, cabbage or cauliflower, every day give you the phytonutrients your body needs to function in top form, keep you well year-around and help prevent cancer. That is a lot of bang for your buck.

Preparing nutrient-dense food does not need to be complicated, time consuming nor expensive. In about the same amount of time it takes for you to warm up the typical frozen dinner, you can cook a small batch of quinoa, cut up and sauté a carrot, some broccoli, four mushrooms and half an onion in a little olive oil, add a splash of Braggs Liquid Aminos—a non-gmo soy product similar to but better for you than soy sauce—or your favorite spices. The result is a meal that is super-healthy and enhances your clarity and creativity.

- **Drink more water.** Seventy-five percent of Americans are chronically dehydrated. Dehydration causes a variety of issues in the body, including but not limited to, headaches, constipation, toxin build up and low energy. Treat water as the amazing health-enhancing elixir that it is. Drink a lot of it. The rule-of-thumb for water consumption is to drink half of your weight in ounces each day. For example, a woman who weighs 130 pounds would consume 65 ounces of water daily.

Dehydration often masks itself as a sugar craving. If you suddenly want something sweet, drink a 12-ounce glass of water and wait ten minutes. It is possible that you are just thirsty, and the craving will pass. A glass or two of water in the afternoon provide a great energy boost. If you aren't crazy about plain water, jazz it up with slices of lemon, lime or cucumber. A re-usable water bottle that has ounces marked on the side is a good investment and a great way to make sure you are getting enough water.

- **Be a super-snacker.** If you find that your body needs a little something at 10:00 a.m. and 3:00 p.m., and you know you are fully hydrated, there's nothing wrong with a healthy snack. A piece of fresh fruit, a handful of almonds or half a cup of hummus with some celery or carrot sticks will do the trick, leaving you satisfied and energized. You can also snack on super foods. These include goji berries, raw cacao nibs, fresh or frozen berries or raw broccoli. These foods are rich in antioxidants and packed with energy.

- **Live by the 90/10 rule.** Ninety percent of the time, eat food that you know is good for you. The other ten percent of the time, eat whatever you want. Yes, this means that once or twice a month you can eat anything. You can't and shouldn't go through life feeling deprived. If your most favorite thing is Cherry Garcia Ice Cream® with chocolate sauce have some occasionally. Eat a reasonable portion and really enjoy it. Pay attention when you eat it and savor every bite. Recognize it as a treat—something special that you eat on occasion. Here's a little warning though: You may find that after eating a healthy diet for a few weeks, these "free" days come at the high cost of low energy, brain fog and an upset digestive system. You may surprise yourself by wanting to give them up!

- **Be the best boss you've ever had.** Remember that a happy you means a prosperous business. Working twelve hours straight is not really productive. After about four hours, unless you are really on a roll, productivity starts to drop. The longer you push on, the worse it gets. Take a break and do something nice for yourself. Brew a cup of herbal tea, take a ten-minute power walk or switch gears by turning on some music that you love and dancing. A dance break is a great way to get re-inspired.

- **Save some of your energy for you each day.** Don't work until you are completely exhausted and then fall into bed. All work and no play make us miserable and that's not why we are here. We are here to be creative and happy. Work until you've accomplished enough to feel good about it, then live a little. Get some exercise, make yourself a healthy, delicious dinner, read a great book, enjoy the company of family and friends, spend some time in silence and get a good night's rest.

- **Enjoy active entertainment every week.** Love yoga? Take a class. Swim like a fish? Find a pool. Is salsa your thing? Get out and shake it. Dreaming of the flying trapeze? There are gyms and teachers. Find your thing and get out there and do it. Active entertainment is great for you on all levels. It is good for your body, mind and spirit—and it is good for your business. You will return to work with a fresh perspective ready to take on what's next.

  If you don't currently have a form of active entertainment that you love, try something new. Join a group of people who already do something you might be interested in. There are groups for all of these activities. Look for them on Craigslist® or in your local community center calendar. Ask around. You'll find them. Get out and have fun!

- **Develop an attitude of gratitude.** Be thankful every day for all the wonderful things in your life. According to Robert Emmon, author of *Thanks!: How the New Science of Gratitude Can Make You Happier* from Houghton Mifflin in 2007, gratitude is scientifically proven to increase your health. A positive attitude will also make you a success magnet and draw your best customers to you. How do you stay positive? Remind yourself that life isn't happening to you. It is happening for you. You get to choose how you react to the circumstances in your life.

  Here is a simple and effective gratitude practice. Each evening after you are in bed and before you fall asleep, think of three things that happened that day you are grateful for. They don't have to be anything big. A flower that you saw, the way the light looked in the early morning or how good your salad tasted at lunch. You'll fall asleep faster and wake up in a good mood, ready to take on the day.

These are some of my best tips. They will only work if you actually do them consistently over time. Pick one or two to implement now.

Which two are your favorites or seem really easy? Stop and think about how you will add them into your life and, more importantly, why. How will it benefit your business if you shift to this new way of being? Be specific. Write it down. It takes six months to integrate a new habit. If you have to start over, do. Eventually your new healthy habits will stick, and then you can pick two more.

Increasing your health will automatically increase the health of your business. If you know that your health needs to improve and are unsure about how to make changes, a holistic health and nutrition coach can help you formulate a plan, establish goals and accomplish them. Just like investing in a software upgrade, investing in a health coach can save you time and increase your productivity. When you are your healthy best you will radiate wellness, inspire others and you and your business will thrive.

Tamara Cameron, HHC, AADP

Holistic Health & Nutrition Coach
FirstLine Therapy Lifestyle Educator
Owner, Health Harvest Holistic Wellness
Cultivating a healthier, happier you!
(415) 602-4174
www.health-harvest.com
tamara@health-harvest.com

Tamara has always been passionate about food, nutrition and balanced living. She learned to be a "foodie" at an early age from her mom, a fabulous cook, and her dad, an avid gardener. Growing up in small-town Idaho, she enjoyed the benefits of "eating local" before local food and farmers' markets became a political issue. She discovered lentils and "brown" bread as a pre-teen and her destiny was set. Since then she has been the "go-to" resource for health and wellness information for her community.

Tamara is passionate about teaching others the joys of a healthy, balanced lifestyle. She specializes in helping busy entrepreneurs make wellness a priority so both they and their businesses thrive.

Tamara presents inspiring, interactive and fun workshops on a variety of holistic health topics both online and in person. She also offers group programs and highly individualized one-to-one nutrition and lifestyle coaching to help people resolve issues that are holding them back from powerfully achieving their goals.

Find a Need in Your Community, Fill It and Make Money

By Alexis Williams-Patton

Never in a million years would I have thought I would be a self-employed individual. Today, it's called "An Entrepreneur." I grew up in a small town where it was popular to go to work for the naval shipyard, work locally if there were jobs or go to college and work in corporate America, which is what I did.

By 1994, my role as a wife and mother changed my outlook about the working world. After I became pregnant, I presented to my boss a telecommuting proposal in an effort to be home with my family. Work and life balance was not popular in the mid-90s, and my request was denied.

I decided to create a "For Profit" business from the ground up. It was birthed out of desperation and, later, the need for survival after going through a divorce. I knew that being your own boss and running your own business was an American dream, so I set out to start one of my own.

All kinds of entrepreneurs have emerged over the past twenty years. There are social entrepreneurs, serial entrepreneurs, tech entrepreneurs, lifestyle entrepreneurs, mommy entrepreneurs and those like me who have become what I have coined a "Social Ill Entrepreneur," a "Do Good Entrepreneur," or a "Help Others Entrepreneur." This is someone who finds a way to solve societal problems, fills a need, and also uses it to create a profitable business by helping others solve a problem in society and getting paid for it.

Your passion or social concern might be homelessness, hunger, compassion to help combat child prostitution, job creation, group homes for wayward teens, day care for burned-out moms, mental health clinics, doggy daycares, companion care for the elderly or even a food truck that provides home-cooked meals for the housebound. Whatever your compassion or passion, it can provide a highly rewarding and lucrative income—most often a six-figure income—if properly planned and leveraged. In this chapter, I am going to show you how to do it with just what you have on a small level. After you read this chapter, I hope that you are encouraged to leverage what you have learned and create a fruitful business for yourself and your family.

"The best way to find yourself is to lose yourself in the service of others."
—Mohandas Ghandi, Indian nonviolent political activist

Do Not Despise Small Beginnings

Search for issues and social ills that are needs, trends or issues with continual societal problems not being addressed or met by your local community, region or state. This is an opportunity to be a blessing to others and find a need and fill it, or to offer a service to fix a particular social problem.

When I started my business, I learned of a need to open residential home health care facilities in the community to help individuals moving out of an institutionalized setting many of which are large state run facilities of 800 or more people. Many people with developmental disabilities have a variety of special needs and don't have coping skills. Some need full support with daily living skills, and others have physical needs that require extra assistance. In the 1980s, a group of parents grew tired of their children with disabilities living in an institutionalized setting and wanted more happiness and freedom for them. They sued the State of of California, which resulted in an agreement to move more than 2,000 people with developmental disabilities into the the community. The goal was to allow individuals to have better opportunities to socialize with friends and family, attend different schools, go to church, go to work, and to be in a normalized non-institutional environment. Individuals were to be placed in smaller home-like settings and given the same opportunities as other citizens. I became very compassionate about this when I heard about this issue. I wanted to do something about it.

Starting a home health care business can be a lot of hard work when you get started. However, over a few short years, it can become a rewarding and lucrative business. Entrepreneur.com maintains that, "13 percent of the population (baby boomers) will have become age 65 by 2010. By 2030, the figure will jump to 19.6 percent."

The need for a non-medical home care industry is booming and residential facilities are needed to accommodate seniors' daily living assistance and companionship. I have found this to be a need with three of my aunts, all of whom are aged 90 and 95 and all of whom are pretty healthy and in their right mind. However, these cute little ladies need help with personal chores done, companionship, housekeeping, transportation and safety management, and they all want to stay in their own homes. Many similar to them want to live in a homelike setting. There are challenging aspects of this business, including taking lots of classes, making a hefty financial investment up front, and obtaining the right licenses to operate your home care business successfully.

I am proud of this business because it has helped to change the lives of those who were developmentally disabled and institutionalized and who wanted to live in a more family-oriented environment. This type of business has also created jobs for the past fifteen years for many women and men who were once on welfare or unemployed.

Starting at the Ground Level

There will be many things you will need, like state and county licensing documentation, employer identification, possibly senior or durable medical equipment, depending on the type of residents you serve, business insurance and a business checking account. You will need a lawyer, banker, insurance agent, and accountant, payroll specialists, advertising campaigns, the ability to work with local regional centers and ombudsman offices, and most importantly, dedicated employees. When I first started, I used students to help me type and put together the enormous amounts of documents and paperwork needed to run a healthcare facility. Today, many resources can be found via the Internet. However, if I were you, I would still use students to help you get started. I am grateful they helped me organize the residential home and assisted me in getting the company off the ground until I had enough capital to hire full-time staff. One of the best things to do before starting out is to find someone doing what you want to do and volunteer. Ask them for help—spend quality time helping them in their business and you can in return learn from them. Continue to bless that person because they could end up becoming a great mentor for you.

I would not advise a new entrepreneur to just step out blindly as I did. It has truly cost me a lot of money. Today, there is a plethora of experts in the land, such as business coaches, mentors and resources to help you reach your goals. Become the protégée of someone else in the business. Find the experts to help you.

Don't be afraid to ask someone for advice. Ask what made them successful. When I started out, I met with more than ten other home health care providers to learn how they ran the business. I also volunteered where the social problems were, so I could get a vision of how to fix them when I started my own business.

Get Started Opening Your Own Home Health Care Business

- Model a local board-and-care home, specialized types of developmentally disabled facilities, elderly care, or other types of home health care facilities in an effort to get an idea of the type of care you will need to provide, such as cooking and preparing healthy meals, taking care of the laundry, dressing, grooming, what it will take to help residents use the bathroom, administering medications, scheduling doctors' appointments, and ensuring that you have the right employees with the compassion for this type of customer you will serve.
- Learn the requirements for your home care facility, such as resident eligibility, meal planning, admission agreements, and transfer and discharge requirements, resident's rights, medication management, Medicare and SSI benefits, physician services, emergency discharge and general care, by contacting your state's licensing department.
- Visit your city planning department and zoning department to assure there is not another facility within 300 feet, and check with neighbors to see if this type of facility is okay to operate within the neighborhood. At least 90 days before your anticipated opening, schedule an inspection with your licensing department.

- Meet with an architect to develop a floor plan that includes the required amenities and safety measures. Apply for a license with your state licensing department. Generally, you will need to include building plans and proof of zoning approval for your proposed location, the application, and three references that can attest to your character and verify your ability to run a residential home care facility.
- Develop an admission agreement for your home care, group home, and elder care facility that details the services provided, visiting hours, and any paid services available, the resident's rights, discharge rights, and refund policies. Establish and document procedures for medications and know how to administer a healthy meal plan, with room for understanding special diets.
- You must purchase general liability and medical malpractice insurance from a provider that specializes in home care. Your current insurance company may be able to connect you with a provider or a network of other care providers to make great referrals.
- Hire a qualified assistant to act in your stead. He or she must meet the state requirements for acting as a manager for a home care business when you are not in the home. If required by your state, hire a licensed nurse to oversee medication procedures. Hire compassionate, friendly and capable employees who can provide care in a dignified manner. All employees are required to undergo a series of classes including first aid and CPR training, medication management training to help employees understand the importance of managing medications, and direct care support services in an effort to realize what it takes to care for a resident on a daily basis.
- Write a comprehensive business plan before submitting any proposals to your state or county's administrator certification board. Get a big binder and divide your business into four main categories: business description, marketing plan, finances and

management. Stick to your business plan and consult with a business mentor/professional to avoid overspending or common pitfall mistakes that can result from improper planning.

- Create your home health care facility name and mission statement. Create a logo, create a brand, develop advertising campaigns and create brochures that define hours/days of operation, and what specific services your home health care facility can provide. You must seek expert help if you do not already know how to do this. Image is everything.
- Many small businesses fail because of the lack of capital. When I started, I took out a $30,000 line of credit. This line of credit helped me maintain the business until it finally began generating an income; in addition, I did *not* quit my day job.
- Make a balance sheet and file all-important documents like loan receipts, cash flow charts and profit-loss and spending, to be aware of how your business is doing. Open a business checking account and consult with an attorney on insurance rates and policies.
- Apply for an employer's identification number through the Internal Revenue Service. You will not be able to serve clients without it. Also, apply for a state seller's permit and a Home Care Agency license. All home health care facilities should have staff trained and certified in CPR and first aid in addition to other classes required by community care licensing, regional centers, and Medi-Cal and Medicare billing resources. Many types of home health care facilities require nursing staff if providing an intermediate skilled nursing type of facility. Some home health care facilities that serve behavioral and mental health residents almost always need psychiatric specialists or technicians, therapists and other licensed professionals.

Making money from doing good, finding a need and filling it has been rewarding for me and my two children as a single mom whose heart's desire was to work closer to home.

We all have God-given gifts and talents. I cannot sing and I was never an athlete, but I love to smile and encourage people. Walt Disney recognized his own strength as a story designer—not the actual animation—so he took his strength along with his brother Roy and grew a multi-billion-dollar empire. You have strength and a gift for something. The world is just waiting for you!

I have been blessed to make more money than I did when I worked in corporate America. In fact, my monthly salary tripled and my gross income doubled. I never, ever thought people could earn more than $100,000 a year, but the sky is the limit on your income when you enter the world as an entrepreneur. How do I know this? I have walked gently in these shoes, and there are others who are treading ground, becoming forerunners and leaving a legacy behind them. Just ask the new billionaires of Silicon Valley.

Today, I am still learning about all of the opportunities available to entrepreneurs. I, like you, am stepping out in faith to encourage other women and men to start small businesses or expand existing ones, provide jobs for others, and answer the call to address a social problem. Join me in doing good for others and reaping the benefits as a social ill entrepreneur.

Alexis Williams-Patton

Alexis Williams Patton Enterprises, LLC

(707) 246-6826
www.alexiswilliamspattonenterprises.com
alexiswilliamspattonauthor@gmail.com

Alexis Williams-Patton is an entrepreneur, mother, healthcare and corporate recruiter consultant, sought-after speaker and published author. As an entrepreneur, she has provided jobs for up to twenty-five women and men. She is the proud founder of "Birth It Out Conferences," "Birthing Out the Dreams God has Placed on the Inside of You" and "Women of Destiny, Purpose and Truth Conferences," a conference that encourages freedom in every area of a woman's life: "Spirit, Soul, and Body."

Alexis uses her books and speaking engagements to help shift, break ground and encourage individuals, women's and men's groups, church groups and college students to birth out the dream and destiny God has placed on the inside of them. She teaches them to promote good will, create jobs for others and use their resources to heal many of the social ills in our communities.

Alexis is completing her master's degree in human resource management and healthcare administration at Golden Gate University, and she holds a bachelor's degree in political science from California State. She has fifteen years of experience as a senior corporate and healthcare recruiter and has worked for many Fortune 500 corporations. She is a proud single mother, raising two academic- and sports-minded teenage sons.

▪ ▪ ▪

Brand Appeal

Your Visual Business Communicator

By Alesia Dowden, MBA, BC

A young woman walked into Tiffany & Co®. It was her first time entering the establishment. She'd heard about the exquisite diamond rings and jewelry and wanted to see them up close and personal. As she entered the foyer, she was greeted by someone with a pleasant smile that welcomed her and made her feel at ease. Lights sparkled above and diamonds twinkled in the display cases below. Her heart raced as she asked the sales person if she could try on a bracelet. As the bracelet was clasped to young woman's wrist, her smile became as bright as the lights shining down on her. After a few minutes of admiring the bracelet, she said, "I will take it."

The salesperson opened a mahogany drawer, pulled out a small, soft teal blue box with a little white bow, placed the bracelet inside and then into a matching bag. As the young woman took the bag, she felt a sense of pride and ownership—she held in her hand a piece of Tiffany—the promise of perfection and elegance. Unknowingly, she held in her hand a well-implemented brand strategy.

One of the most enjoyable moments of developing and growing your business will occur as you embark upon branding your product or service or when you are creating a personal brand. Whether you design your own brand or hire a professional, this is the moment in which your creativity must flourish. You will be challenged to merge all aspects of your business into a visual presentation and create a signpost that reads, "Stop here. I have what you need." You will place your business on the map of the business world and in the minds of the consumer.

"The quality of your work, in the long run, is the deciding factor on how much your services are valued by the world."
—Orison Swett Marden, American author and founder of Success Magazine

Brand Elements

When branding your product or service, you need to be creative and to construct a strategic branding plan. Your plan will encompass several components, such as how you will interact with the consumer, find and attract clients, how you are different from your competitor, your company's foundation and pledge to its clients. Within your strategic plan, you need to incorporate several important brand elements: your company name, logo, tagline, colors and graphics. Pinpoint your target audience and then form a visual bond through shapes and colors.

First Impressions—Your Logo

Image is everything when it comes to developing your logo.

Your logo is a visual graphic that allows the consumer to identify your specific product or service. Consumers must see or hear a marketing message several times before they will act on it. The mind will often play back an image or a message before connecting it to a name. This is why your logo plays an important role in the branding process.

It does not matter whether your business is large or small, your logo may be the defining symbol that causes customers to select your product or service versus the other company around the corner. Think creatively when developing your logo and remember to incorporate the essence of your business into it. Incorporating the essence of your business will require you to relay a message without speaking a word—shapes, colors and words must tell your business story. For example, if you own a jewelry business, you would not choose a picture of a cat unless the jewelry is for animals. To clearly express to the consumer that the product you provide is jewelry, your logo might be a ring or a pearl necklace.

If you gave your customers a free t-shirt with your logo on it, would they actually wear it or would it sit in the bottom of their dresser drawer?

Your branding goal is to cause your customers to connect with you on many levels and become passionate about your product or service to the degree that they are willing to liberally promote your product or service. You might want to include this question on your next customer survey in an effort to understand your brand appeal. Remember, most of your sales will come from repeat customers and from those they refer to you.

Over time, your logo may change as you refine your business purpose. However, be careful not to change your image drastically to the point where your current clients lose image connectivity and must re-identify with your product or service. Subtle changes to your logo are best unless you are introducing an entirely different business. You may recall that Coca-Cola® tried reinventing the wheel by changing the look of their cans and the taste of their product as their competitor Pepsi® started to claim more shelf space. You may also remember that Coca-Cola failed considerably and reverted to the basics.

What Your Tagline Says about Your Business

If you could tell someone about your business in just a few words that would motivate them to respond immediately, what would you say? This is what your tagline or catch phrase does. It gives the consumer a glimpse of what your business is about, promotes your company's values and beliefs and causes the consumer to take action. Your tagline will be placed on all advertising or marketing tools to cause the consumer to be drawn to your product or service simply by identifying with your brand slogan.

Smart taglines include three major components: your promise, purpose and passion. Conveying a message that encompasses all three components will require revising several times. Before developing your tagline, jot down a clear and concise answer for each of the three components.

1. What is your customer promise?
2. What is your purpose?
3. What are you passionate about concerning your business?

With a clear picture of what your business has to offer the consumer, you will be able to create a tagline with substance and one that conveys benefits to the consumer.

Your tagline is most important when developing your brand, as it allows the consumer to connect with you on an emotion level. Remember when Nike® said, "Just do it"? That three-word phrase changed the thinking of the consumer on many planes and took away all excuses not to succeed. People began to take risks and step outside of their comfort zones.

Can you create a tagline that does the same? Sure, you can! Entrepreneurs are crafting phrases that draw the consumer to the products and services on a continual basis.

My personal tagline is *Dream Big & Think Smart*. The majority of my clients are new to small business ownership. They have dreams of doing great things and making millions of dollars. However, many entrepreneurs would crash and burn right out of the door because their dream is often too big for them to grasp in its totality. My goal is to help the entrepreneur manage their dream and make it a reality. My goal is to make the entrepreneur think about what they are trying to accomplish and perform their tasks with wisdom to save time and money.

Personal Branding

Whether you know it or not, if you are selling any type of product or service to your clients on a continuous basis, you have already begun phase one of personal branding. Personal branding starts when customers begin to identify or connect you with the product or service you provide. For example, women who sell cosmetics such as Avon® or Mary Kay® are often called "the Avon Lady" or "the Mary Kay Lady." Their clients associate the product with the person bringing a new and personal identity to the entrepreneur. However, should you choose to take personal branding to the next level so that you become the brand, prepare to become an expert in your field as well.

Personal branding is becoming more common today, as entrepreneurs find that it is often easier to brand one's self versus a business. As an entrepreneur, you understand more about yourself, your capabilities and your beliefs, and are therefore able to promote and market yourself with ease. Identifying yourself as an expert in your field will be your primary task as you begin building your personal brand. This can be done through several means:

1. Get involved in your community and become a voice. Joining the chamber of commerce in your city can be a great help—such organizations are designed to connect business owners to their community. Most chambers have some type of newsletter or e-mailer and are often in need of articles for publication. This is the perfect opportunity for you to be exposed to the public, get free advertisement and become noted as a published writer.

2. Use the media to become a community celebrity or activist. What do you stand for? Call your local cable company to find out if there are any panels that promote your field of expertise. If so, do a little research to find out how you can become a panel member. Area newspapers are also a great place to begin promoting your expertise. You can host an event and advertise in your local newspapers.

3. Become an Internet sensation. Entrepreneurs are using the Internet to get the word out, be discovered and become noticed for their knowledge. There are many resources available to do this, such as your personal website, YouTube®, Internet radio and webinars.

The more you promote yourself and become a well-known figure in the community, the more people and organizations will begin to seek you out for your expertise and knowledge. Remember, credibility goes a long way and, while any publicity is good publicity, you should prefer positive exposure. Positive exposure will benefit your personal brand much more than negative exposure.

Creativity Counts

Creativity is extremely important as you begin the branding process because cookie-cutter branding does not always work for every business. It is much better to stretch your imagination and think outside the box to create something original, fresh and new. Today's consumer is armed with information and will quickly realize a copycat when they see one. For example, has anyone ever given you his or her business card, and you noticed that you have seen it before? This is especially common at large business conferences.

Take time to discover the precise message you want to convey about your product or service and design a brand that will cause the consumer to react!

A requirement for each of my clients as we begin the branding phase of their business is to perform a brand search on the Internet. They are required to locate six or more related businesses and dissect the brand. They must then tell me what they saw, felt and experienced while reviewing the sites.

This exercise helps you discover what is already in the market and how you do not want your business to be perceived visually. You will also begin to understand how colors, shapes, words and sounds impact and influence the customer's shopping habits.

Dissecting other companies' brands and understanding how consumers are influenced to purchase can be of great assistance when developing your brand strategy. Not only do you need to pay close attention to colors and shapes for your brand, you will also need to become creative with your written message. When creating your tagline, give your clients a catchy phrase to remember without them thinking about it.

Do It Yourself or Hire a Specialist

Making the decision as to whether you should develop your brand on your own or hire a professional graphic designer could actually determine the fate of your business. Remember, your brand should reflect the personality and characteristics of your business and the primary message you want to relay to the consumer. Although every entrepreneur believes they are somewhat creative as they have developed a unique product or service, know your creative limitations when it comes to design, design placement and color.

If you happen to be an entrepreneur that has creative abilities and are computer savvy, you will more than likely want to take on developing your brand on your own. Developing your brand can be done quite easily. The market is flooded with logo design software, and the Internet offers a host of service providers that offer simple branding solutions, such as matching business cards, stationery and websites. Your personal computer and the applications on it will also come in handy in developing your brand. For example, Microsoft PowerPoint® can be a very useful tool when you are designing your logo.

Working with a professional graphic designer has its disadvantages as well as advantages. A few of the disadvantages are time and money. Depending on the designer's schedule, you may be required to wait a few weeks before a design is made from your rough draft and then a few more weeks before it is finalized. The entire process may also be somewhat costly, depending on the techniques used to design your logo.

Be prepared to go back to the drawing board several times before you actually get it right. However, the advantage of hiring a professional graphic designer is that your final product will be a clear and crisp design that will exemplify the essence of your business.

There are several avenues you can take when selecting a good graphic designer. Check your local phonebook to find a list of graphic designers in your area, and talk with business owners who have used graphic designers to design their brand and search the Internet. Whichever avenue you select to find a graphic designer, make sure to review samples of their work and get references. The best graphic designer will keep the communication line open and allow you to have creative control of your design.

"It's choice not chance that determines your destiny."
—Jean Nidetch, American business personality
and motivational speaker

Take Your Time

Colors, shapes and messages—they all count. You cannot leave any part of your branding elements to chance. Each element must be designed with purpose and geared to reach your specific audience.

Your ultimate goal when branding your product or service is to ensure that your business message stays inside the thoughts of the consumer. This is a process that should not be rushed—you are holding your business's future and perceived credibility in the palm of your hands. Remember, your name, logo and tagline will be placed on every piece of marketing material you develop, so make it count.

Color will play a major role in the development of your brand. I would like to suggest you start the branding process by gaining understanding of the psychology of color. Perform a quick search on the Internet, type in "psychology of color," and you will find a host of information that will provide insight as to which color will influence your target audience. Market researchers continuously perform studies and spend thousands of dollars yearly to understand the relationship between color and consumer response.

Take the opportunity to use all of your resources, family, friends and branding experts. Survey your target audience, if possible. Share your branding idea with your mastermind group or your business coach, as this will allow you to talk it through and discover your brand style. Most of all, do your research. Keep in mind that the effort you put into your branding strategy may very well drive more customers to your door.

Alesia Dowden, MBA, BC

Alesia Dowden Enterprise

Dream Big & Think Smart

(661) 208-6015
alesia.dowden@yahoo.com
www.alesiadowden.com

Alesia Dowden is the owner and "Extreme Business Coach" of Alesia Dowden Enterprise, a business dedicated to assisting the new entrepreneur in developing and fine-tuning their home-based business. She believes that most people have hidden talents that can produce financial well-being when properly cultivated.

Alesia has worked for a major corporation for the past 22 years as a senior program financial analyst, offering upper-level management teams alternative solutions to cost issues. Her expertise is turning matters of chaos into streamlined processes.

In 2002, Alesia began her first entrepreneurial venture. She merged her analytical and business skills with her creative crafting skills and started a home-based business. As she began to share the story of how she overcame financial obstacles through home-based business ownership, she discovered more women just like her who required business guidance. She is now on a mission to assist women entrepreneurs develop and grow their home-based businesses by leading the way. Her field of study at the University of Phoenix is business management. She holds bachelor of science and master of business administration degrees.

■ ■ ■

Plan Before You Build

Things to Consider for New and Existing Websites

By Win Day

A website can be a powerful tool in your marketing toolkit. It can also be one of the largest single expenses that your business incurs. If your website is not getting the results you want, if it is not growing your list and making you money, take a close look at your design, your content and your strategy. On the other hand, if your business does not yet have a website, what are you waiting for?

Use these concepts when you are having a new website developed or when you are reviewing your existing website. The result will be a website that is built on a solid foundation and supports your business growth and prosperity.

Establish Your Purpose and Goals

Put time and effort into the planning stage. The more clearly you can identify what you want on the website, the more precisely a web developer can match your vision. The more thought you put into what you want for the future, the easier it will be for the website to change and grow as your business changes and grows. Think about long-term goals as well as immediate needs.

What do you want this website to accomplish? Is it meant to inform, to educate, to entertain, to sell? The website's goals will have a major impact on the content you include and the writing style you use for that content.

How will having this website, new or improved, impact your business? Do you expect more sales, fewer customer service phone calls, or maybe new investors or advertisers? Set measurable targets for these business results. Over time, you will be able to figure out the effectiveness—the return on investment—of the website.

What do you want your audience to be able to do on the website? Can they purchase online, or print off an order form to fax or mail in? Do you want them to call you for more information? Are you trying to build an online community with your audience? The visitor activities that you build in will drive the website's contents and structure.

Consider Your Schedule and Budget

What is your timeframe for this project? Do you have a target launch date in mind that has to match up with a special event?

Do you have all or most of your content ready? The most common speed bump I encounter on website projects is clients who underestimate the amount of time that they need to plan, create, and review their content.

Your web developer will also have schedule considerations. He or she has other projects and other clients, and needs to work on his or her own business. The elapsed time required for a project, the time between project kickoff and the launch date has to consider all these things.

What is your budget for this project? One of the first questions I hear from potential clients is, "How much will this cost?" I need a great deal of information before I can provide an estimate.

Would you walk up to a real estate agent and say, "I want to buy a piece of property," giving them no more information than that, and expect an answer that makes sense? You need to tell him whether you want to buy a residential, commercial or industrial property. How big is the parcel? Do you need a building on it? How big? What kind of building? Your real estate agent needs to know the answers to those questions and many more before he or she can even start looking. Website projects have just as many variables, all of which contribute to the cost.

A do-it-yourself website, built using the web-building wizard at your hosting company, may cost you no more than the hosting fee plus your time. (Please do recognize that your time has a real cost.) An e-commerce website like Amazon.ca probably cost millions of dollars. Your website will fit somewhere in between the two extremes.

Where it fits on that cost spectrum will depend on considerations such as how big the website is (how much content, in how many sections), what it needs to do, how it needs to work, what content or information still needs to be created or sourced, and what other services you might need, such as audio or video or graphics creation.

Set Up Your Domain Registration and Hosting

Before the actual development starts, register a domain and set up hosting.

Your domain name is the way browsers and search engines connect to you. It is like a phone number you can choose, or a vanity license plate. Since you get to choose it, make it mean something. Use your company name, or the name of the product or service that the website features.

A hosting account is rented space on a computer that connects to the Internet. What kind of hosting you need depends on what your website will contain and what it will do. A five-page brochure website needs less storage space or bandwidth (how much will transfer to and from your website in a month) than a photographer's portfolio website that has thousands of large pictures, or a coach's website that has many training videos and articles. If you intend to use any sort of third party application such as a content management system (I strongly recommend WordPress®) or a shopping cart, you will also need a database to go along with file storage space. Then there is email, backups, statistics and all sorts of other features to consider before choosing a hosting company.

Figure out in advance what your website needs to do before locking into a hosting agreement that you may outgrow before the end of the contract. In my experience, it is best to choose a host that is neither a very large company nor a very small one. Large hosts such as phone and cable companies tend to put many websites on one server, which means your website has to fight for resources. Very small companies may appeal to you because you met the owner at a networking event, but do you really want to depend on someone with a couple of computers in his basement?

Choose a host that sits comfortably in the middle. You want one large enough to provide a good hosting environment (powerful computers, redundant or mirrored servers in case one fails, physical security at the location) and small enough to provide good personal service.

Define Your Audience

Whom is the website for? Hint: it is not for you, and it is not for your web developer. Whom do you want the website to attract?

Who they are affects why they visit and what they expect to find and do when they get there. Who they are determines the content (what is included and what is not included), the functionality (how the information is organized, what visitors can do), and the style (who it appeals to).

Before you start planning your website, sort out your branding. You want to define your target market, your offerings (products and services) and your messaging.

Consider that your customers—those who use your products and services—may not necessarily be the intended audience for this website—or at least not the only audience. Does the website also need to draw investors, joint venture partners or sponsors? Do you need to have a secure private area for your staff, shareholders or other members?

Determine Functionality Requirements

Your website purpose drives its functionality. How the website works and what your visitors can do there will depend on what you are trying to accomplish.

Whether you work with a web developer or create the website yourself, think about what the website needs to do. Think about today, think about tomorrow and think about the future. You may not build in all the bells and whistles right from the start, but if you know that down the road you will include a photo gallery, or a forum, or a membership area, plan for it now. If your website is built with expansion in mind, it will serve you for a much longer time without having to be rebuilt from scratch.

What do you want your visitors to do there? I strongly encourage you to include both a blog and an email newsletter subscription form that is tied to your irresistible *free offer*. Will you sell directly from the website? Do you offer audio or video on your site, paid or free, for visitors to download?

Create Your Content

Content is all the bits and pieces that are contained in the framework of the visual design, and that bring your visitors back again and again.

Your content derives from your purpose and aims at your audience. Make it clear, concise and compelling.

With your purpose and audience firmly in mind, outline your content. That outline becomes the structure or organization of your website, and will quickly reveal where you have enough (or too much) content and where you need to do some work.

Hire a writer or a marketer or both if you are not comfortable writing it yourself. If you do write your own content, make sure someone else reads it carefully. This is important stuff here—do not leave it to chance.

Make sure every page, every chunk of content, serves the purpose of the website. If it does not, think long and hard about whether you really need to put that content online. Alternatively, at the very least, put non-essential content deeper into the website. Interested readers will poke around to find it, and readers that are more casual will not be distracted from the primary function of the website.

You will most likely use an overall organization something like this:

- Home
- About
- Blog—may be sorted into categories
- Products—may be sorted into categories
- Services—may be sorted into categories
- Contact

You may have other bits and pieces, such as:

- Events—may be displayed as a calendar or a list
- Galleries
- Testimonials
- Affiliate or partner programs
- Member areas

You will also need some pages or areas for the underlying legal content that needs to be on your website but does not need to be front and center:

- Privacy policy
- Disclaimers—for testimonials, or claims of possible earnings or achievements
- Terms of service—shipping, returns, warranties

Design the Layout

The visual design of your website is the framework that holds all the content. It is what makes that all-important first impression, and should accurately reflect the image you want to portray.

The more thought you put into the visual design up front, and the more clearly you can convey your preferences, the better your web developer or graphic designer will be able to match the result to your vision. Even if you choose to use a pre-built template, plan in advance how you want the site to look and feel.

Build For Usability

Here is where form follows function. While the visual design is important for that first impression, do not let a visual design get in the way of your message. Your visitors want to use your website, not just look at it.

Use Appropriate Technology

Be cautious about implementing the latest and greatest technologies merely for the sake of doing so. There are many appropriate uses for Flash and other "special effects," but ninety percent of them are worthless. Follow the KISS (Keep It Simple, Sweetie) principle.

Do not get cute and clever with the navigation! Search engines do not like it, screen readers for the visually impaired do not like it, cell phones and other mobile devices do not like it, and your audience will not like it. It is possible to build visually beautiful menus—and indeed entire sites—that are valid, accessible, and search engine friendly.

If you will have large audio or video files, consider hosting them on a website that is set up to host and deliver them, such as Amazon S3. You will not be caught short because your own server type or hosting package cannot support the file size or bandwidth required to serve them up to your hungry audience.

Address Accessibility

This generally means, but is not limited to, making sure your website is accessible to the visually impaired. It is far easier and less expensive to build it in from the beginning than to retrofit and add it later.

For more information on accessibility testing and guidelines, see www.contentquality.com.

Test Before You Launch

Test, test, test. You simply cannot test enough. Test in the working environment by putting the website on the server where it will be hosted, even if it is in a protected area or a hidden subdomain until it goes live.

Test your website in various browsers on both major platforms. Consider creating a mobile-friendly version of your website for cell phones and tablets.

Chances are you will not have access to different browsers and platforms. There is an online service www.browsercam.com that allows you to test on all sorts of browser and operating systems and mobile devices.

Think About the Extras

Much of your content is likely to be text, or a combination of text and images. What else does your website need in order to convert casual visitors into repeat visitors, and repeat visitors into paying customers?

These are some elements of highly successful websites:

- **An email newsletter subscription form.** You do send out an email newsletter, right? Use a third party service such as Constant Contact®

(www.constantcontact.com) or 1ShoppingCart® (www.1shoppingcart.com) to manage and distribute your email newsletter. These services will make sure that opt-in subscribes and unsubscribes and bounces are handled correctly and legally.

- **An irresistible free offer.** I get hundreds of messages to my inbox every week. Why would I subscribe to your newsletter? What high-value content can you give to visitors to get them to subscribe?
- **Video.** People do business with those they know, like, and trust. When you do business online, you have to work harder to create that trust connection than you do when you network in person. Video is a powerful tool for putting a face and character to your website. The videos do not have to be high-end, high-cost productions. Use your webcam to record some of your articles or blog posts, so that your visitors can get a taste of you and what you offer.
- **Internal links.** Google® dearly loves internal links—links between pages or posts within your website. If a piece of content is important enough to link to it from somewhere else within the site, Google thinks it is important too.
- **A strong call to action.** Yes, this is text, but this is the one piece I see missing from so many websites. Tell them what you want them to do. People are not dumb, but they are busy. If they cannot figure out what to do next, they will not do anything at all. Make it glaringly obvious what their next step is, whether that is to click a Buy Now button, or to follow a Read More link, or to pick up the phone and call you.

Take Action Now

- **Review your current website yourself.** If you already have a website, review it with the items in this article in mind. Look at every page, every chunk of content. Make sure that what you have online is consistent with and supports the rest of your marketing.

- **Have someone else review your website.** Ask a current or past client. Ask a business colleague. Ask someone you met at a networking event.
- **Hire a web strategist.** You may need professional help with this step. It is not easy to effectively and dispassionately review our own material. If your website has not been reviewed in more than a year, or if you do not have a website, work with someone who can guide you through the process.

Do it now. Do it regularly. The result will be a website that is built on a solid foundation and supports your business by growing your list and making you money.

Win Day

Creative Implementations

Web Strategy Made Easy

(866) 200-1088
Win@CreativeImplementations.com
www.CreativeImplementations.com

Married since 1980 and mother of two wonderful sons, Win Day left the corporate world in 1992 and never looked back. Win's diverse background includes her career as a chemical engineer, marketing coordinator for a large engineering firm, freelance technical writer, multi-media program graduate, successful small business owner, web strategist and WordPress® web developer.

Win's project management, writing and marketing experience, coupled with her strong communication and technical skills, provide a solid foundation for her to build Creative Implementations and to help you build your business.

As a web strategist, Win bridges the gap between the technical, "geeky" side of web development—and the graphic designers, virtual assistants, marketing consultants, search engine optimization consultants and other web developers who might be involved in the projects—and the entrepreneurs who need a website that works for them, for their clients and for their business. Her straightforward, non-technical presentations and workshops on web and content strategy reassure her clients that their website, as a powerful part of their marketing toolkit, will help grow their list and make them money.

Relational Marketing

The Power of Blending Face-to-Face with Online Networking

By Kym Glass

We have heard through the years that it takes a village to raise a child. The same is true of building your own entrepreneurial business. It takes a connected community to help you to build, grow and sustain your business in today's marketplace.

As an entrepreneur, it is difficult to wear all the hats you must wear for your business and network, lead generate and cold call to find ideal clients. Because business starts with relationship building, it is important to begin networking while building loyalty, trust and friendship with potential prospects. These people will be more likely to assist you by either using your product and service or trusting you enough to refer you to others that may be seeking your expertise. The importance of networking is that you must continuously identify ideal prospects and clients to keep your sales funnel alive.

People do business with people, not companies. Networking is one of the most important key ingredients to begin and sustain the longevity of your business. It is important as a business owner to be seen because people want to connect directly with the people they want to do business with.

Face-to-Face Relational Marketing

Whether you are new and launching your business or just need to refocus on the face-to-face relational marketing area of your business, there are three keys that should always remain top-of-mind for opening doors and building collaboration for your business growth. They are:

- Know me
- Like me
- Trust me

It is important to have these keys working properly in your business to build rapport with potential prospects and clients, so others have the opportunity to learn more about you and your business and how they can assist you.

I have personally used the Know Me-Like Me-Trust Me formula to gather over 15,000 connections. I know first-hand these components are "must haves" in your marketing portfolio for forming new business connections, strategies and alliances with others. Know Me-Like Me-Trust Me is not about sell, sell, sell. People want to connect with you first, build a good relationship, learn more about your business and understand their need for your product and service before buying from you.

Get Started Networking

There are several events in your local area where you can learn proper face-to-face relational marketing protocol for growing and enhancing your role as a business owner—local chambers of commerce, professional networking events and nonprofit events.

I began learning to network while working in the telecommunications industry. My executive and mentor, Dale Booth, asked me to attend the local chamber of commerce events, meet community leaders and build rapport with them.

After a chamber event, I would return to the office with business cards and meet with my staff to discuss each of the connections made and provide feedback from the event. My team made calls, set appointments and completed transactions because of the connections made on behalf of the company. I was thrilled to have been given this opportunity. I discovered how passionate I am about connecting and assisting others in their businesses.

If attending events is not comfortable for you, I would recommend you attend with a mentor, friend or acquaintance, or use a networking buddy system to help you until you become more comfortable. Remember: no one knows your company better than you do, so you are your best asset!

Once you attend one or two events, you will be on your way to thriving in one of the most exciting and empowering arenas for building your business and your brand.

Your Thirty-or-Sixty Second Commercial

Think of your thirty- or sixty-second commercial as your personal TV commercial. Create a buzz and excitement for your business!

Whether you are meeting with one person, a small group or are part of a large meeting, the four key pieces of information that people specifically want to know are:

- **Your name**—"Hello, my name is Kym Glass."
- **Your company name and niche offering**—"I am 'The People Person,' Konnector and Konduit. I offer strategic global business connections, sales support and marketing services and have amazing talent in my speaker's bureau for keynotes, events or workshop opportunities."
- **Who is an ideal client for you:** "Anyone who has tasks on their back burner that are preventing them from doing what they are best at in their business. For example, everyone hates cold calling except me. I would enjoy assisting your business by making calls and getting appointments booked for you with your target market."
- **What do you need or what is your business challenge**—"I'm looking for three sponsors that would enjoy national media attention for a speaking tour I'm coordinating with the bureau that I represent."

I would encourage you to be specific in what you need. Genuine people will want to know how they can help you. Remember: people cannot assist you unless you ask and are very specific about your needs.

You may also want to think about an even shorter version of your commercial. There are occasions you will chat with someone briefly and may only have ten to fifteen seconds to make an impression. You want to stand out and make sure you are memorable, even though your time may be limited.

For example: "Hello, I'm Kym Glass 'The People Person.' What is your business and how can I help you with locating an ideal business referral for you?"

Online Relational Marketing

As with face-to-face relational marketing, whether you are just launching your business or working to add business social media exposure, online relational marketing provides another top-of-mind awareness in these three key areas:

- Engage me
- Entertain me
- Educate me

One of the key elements that should be very clear is that, for the best results, you should connect in the face-to-face relational marketing arena prior to online relational marketing. It is possible to connect online first. However, the best protocol is to be mutually introduced by another connection first or have at least seventy-five mutual online connections prior to connecting online.

With online relational marketing, the protocols are quite different. Remember, "nothing goes away, even if you delete it," so be very careful and think clearly before posting. Another caution is to be careful what you post online, as you may get more engagement feedback than you cared to receive and sometimes it may even be inappropriate. As you are your own brand, online relational marketing should always be utilized in a professional manner in all areas, including Facebook®, Twitter®, LinkedIn®, YouTube® and so on.

While you generally have thirty seconds to make a good impression with face-to-face relational marketing, you have much less time in the online relational marketing realm when it comes to being professional about you and your business!

How to Give and Receive Referrals

Choose to be a giver, as opposed to thinking what is in it for me. As you meet others and hear their business introduction commercial, think about your mental Rolodex® and who you know that may be a great lead for them. When you think of a referral, turn your business card over and write the referral person's name on your card and pass it to the person with whom you wish to share the referral connection. The reason for this is so that after your initial meeting, they can follow up with you to obtain additional contact information for the referral that you recommended to them.

In relational marketing, the wisest thing you can do is to share your resources, tools and support. The buzz for my business came from this concept of continually giving meaningful referrals at events. I became the go-to person and in doing so, the passion and purpose for building my own business became a reality.

The greatest asset to both face-to-face and online relational marketing is that your connections and meaningful referrals become your sphere of influence. As an example, I have clients that I met online as the result of a referral from someone else. Because of this relational marketing capability, your sphere of influence can go in multiple directions or in a perfect circle in the face-to-face or online relational marketing areas, depending on how you were introduced to your connection.

Understanding and using your sphere of influence is the real beauty of using relational marketing to its fullest potential. This concept is not only rewarding, but I have created some of the greatest business connections and lifelong friendships by using this methodology.

Following Up and Following Through

The fun and fortune is all in your follow-up! You generally receive an average of seven to nine no responses before you get a yes. After meeting someone at an event or having been introduced by another, it is important to have a one-on-one follow-up meeting in person or with a conference call to learn more specifics about them and their business.

You gain in-depth insights about their business, and they gain knowledge about you and your business. Remember: this is not a one-sided conversation, and you both will leave with a better understanding of each other's business, niche market and ideal clients. You will also better understand:

- Are they a good strategic fit for your business or for someone you know?
- What is the size and width of their sphere of influence?
- Would you ultimately spend your money with them?
- Are they a good referral source?
- Do they come from a place of "giving" or "taking?"

At the conclusion of this meeting, you may want to let them know that you would enjoy being connected with them on Facebook®, Twitter® or LinkedIn® and if so, provide them with information on the best online method for you to stay connected.

Key Connecting Ingredients and Action Steps

Here are some key connecting ingredients that I have developed along the way to enhance my own business relational marketing success. It is my hope that these will assist you on your business journey as well.

Remember, always *show up as you!*

People want to see you in your own true and transparent authenticity. Eight percent of your success is achieved simply by showing up!

- Show up with your 30/60 second commercial fine-tuned.
- Show up with confidence.
- Show up with energy.
- Show up confident and knowing your business niche.
- Show up to inspire someone to want to know more about your business.
- Show up in your purpose, power and passion!

Be Present with your Intentions. Do not be distracted, and stay strategically focused!

- Be in the present moment.
- Focus on what you are specifically looking to gain from attending an event.
- Decide what you need today.
- Find out how you can help someone.
- Identify who needs to know you.

Support Your Business Connections. Think before you buy!

- Purchase from within your referral network.
- Refer others to your connections.
- Track the amount of business you have referred to others.

Be grateful. Always be grateful and thankful to those who have entrusted you with a lead or referral. They could be sharing with you your next top client, and you cannot afford to let them down. My most valuable business cards are those that have been given to me with a referral name written on the back. I never forget anyone who has given me a referral and I remind them frequently how blessed and appreciative I am to have them in my referral network.

Use Snail Mail. Send an occasional note card in the mail. We are so inundated with emails and technology that I enjoy sending and receiving note cards in the mail. Send a note to those you just met, with whom you have a one-on-one conversation, to thank someone for a referral or to acknowledge a special celebratory day. Again, this is a great, top-of-mind, awareness action that people enjoy and rarely forget.

Use Relational Marketing to Build Your Business

Relational marketing is a powerful concept and process if applied in the right way. The relational marketing model is all about people and processes. It is the process of giving before getting and making sure that everything is focused on the simple fact that people do business with people and not with companies!

It is about a strategic, systematic and focused way to process information, listen to clients and be attentive to their needs, wants and concerns first before getting them to engage with the people in your business or non-profit organization. Here is a simple step process of what you need to learn from your clients so that you know how to effectively use relational marketing to build your business into action:

- Understand what their next year growth, goals and objectives are.
- Understand what their business challenges and pains are.
- Understand what their focus is and what they may be looking to diversify in their business offerings.

Relational Marketing is the perfect strategy employed to bring the face-to-face and online communication and engagement together. These two very powerful forces should be used by every business to create and deliver superior value to its prospects and clients.

Kym Glass

Konnector—Konduit

(469) 999-8711
www.kymglass.com
kym@kymglass.com

Kym Glass is a seasoned entrepreneur and natural global business connector, which is why she is called "The People Person" and is a powerhouse business *konnector and konduit*. She is a sought-after speaker for networking facilitation, relational marketing, basic networking principles, key ingredients to your business success and her personal story of unshakeable courage . . . from chaos to clarity.

Prior to beginning her own business to assist entrepreneurs, small to medium-sized business owners and corporations network and connect more effectively, she spent more than twenty years in the telecommunications industry. She has expertise in executive administration management, organizational development, customer service, people value, office management, administration leadership, project management, process management and human resources.

Kym has the innate ability to bring out the best in everyone she meets. When you meet her, you instantly "get" the concept of six degrees of separation and see her genuine warmth and passion for assisting others.

Creating Information Products to Expand Your Success

By Dortha Hise

Entrepreneurs wear many hats in business. From networking and client calls, to social media and newsletter creation, entrepreneurs are some of the busiest people that I know. For entrepreneurs, it is important to create a steady pipeline of new prospects and clients to maintain your cash flow in your business. Product creation may not be one of the hats that you have thought to try on. Over the next few pages, I will share different types of information products and identify key ones to incorporate into your business to begin making money immediately! I will also include tips to monetize each information product. A resource list is also included to help guide you on your information product journey.

There are physical products and information products. A physical product is anything you tangibly hold in your hand, such as a book or a DVD. Alternatively, an information product is anything digital that can be downloaded from your website or emailed to the person who orders it. Typically, what you will see on a website is "Click here to download your XYZ copy of our Special Report," and you enter your email address to receive the report. A moment later, the special report is in your email inbox. One key thing with any product, whether physical or information, you want to provide value for the people who will ultimate be downloading or purchasing it, so they want to come back and experience more of you.

Types of Information Products

Some examples of information products include blogs, articles, newsletters, eBooks, tele-classes, webinars, podcasts, videos and special reports. I will take a few moments to explain each of these and then share how to create your own information products.

The beauty of information products is that they can build on each other. For example, once you create a blog, you can expand on your points to create an article, which is longer than your blog. Likewise, your articles can become features of your newsletter or be compiled into chapters of an eBook and so on.

Blogs

A blog is like a journal except it is published to the world. Your entries are called "posts," and people can subscribe to your posts, make comments on your blog and create an entire community around your following. Many blogs focus on one particular topic; others are more of an online journal similar to a diary. Others are incorporated into a company's branding and utilized as advertising. Blogs include text content, images and, sometimes, links to other blogs or websites to keep the content fresh and up-to-date. If you are in business, a blog is a great tool to have in your marketing arsenal.

According to a study by The Nielsen Company (www.nmincite.com), as of February 2011, over 156 million public blogs existed on the Internet. It warrants repeating: If you are in business, a blog is a great tool to have. There are several online resources to create your blog online. Two such sites are WordPress.com® or Blogger.com®, which are both free.

Another beautiful thing that you can do with blogging is become a guest blogger. You can search for blogs that are a match to your ideal clients and ask about writing a blog for them. What you may find is that some bloggers provide compensation for this and the exposure to an entirely new list of people may be the reward for you in this endeavor. See "Using Blogs and Video to Build Your Business" by Robin Smith on page 175.

Articles

An article can be produced in either print or electronic format. For the purposes of this discussion, we will focus on the electronic version of an article.

An article is often a minimum of 500 words and various article directory sites online have different requirements. If you decide you are going to utilize articles as an information product and use proliferation as a method of getting your word out, make sure you check the editorial guidelines when submitting for word count, topic and so on. One client I work with creates an article a month and then circulates the content to many article directory sites as well as doing outreach to physical publications to see if they have a need for articles. The beauty of the physical publications is that some of them pay!

Let's say you are a business coach and you have created an article called "Ten Tips for Business Success." Once you come up with the title of your article, you begin creating each paragraph or section. Give lots of ideas and tips and incorporate client experiences and testimonials to help support each point.

You can really gain momentum in proliferation of your articles and get your name out there with article directories. They allow you to post your article in one place with the potential of thousands of other sites seeing your article and having them post your article on their site. Make sure to read the fine print when using article directories as there may be exclusivity and other things that you may not want to grant when posting to various places.

Newsletters

A newsletter is a form of direct marketing that is sent to folks who are subscribed to your list. A newsletter incorporates articles, ads, tips and more. Your newsletter is a way to stay in front of your subscribers. After someone comes to your website and opts in for your free report or eBook, the newsletter is the next way to stay top-of-mind for your prospects.

One client came to me and had never done a newsletter. We set up a beautiful template in Constant Contact® and began doing a weekly newsletter post that he incorporated into his blog. We are regularly posting his materials throughout social media, and he is getting new clients because of being in front of his target market on a regular basis.

The monetizing of your newsletter really comes from the reputation you build among your followers and if they are sharing your newsletter with others. Are you getting it out on social media? You could also tie in a special offer just for your newsletter subscribers—for example, a discounted rate for your new ebook! In providing a ton of value in your newsletter content, people will want to work more with you, and they come into the funnel of your information products on the store of your website.

eBooks

An eBook is an electronic version of a book that can be read on a computer or smart device. It can vary in length from five pages to a full-length novel or book. It is sometimes a free downloadable at your opt-in box on your website. It can include images and diagrams, as in a hard copy book, except it is electronic.

After you have created an article, you can extrapolate your material and expand on each piece to create a chapter for each step you discussed in the article, thus creating your eBook. I have helped many clients create an eBook as a starting point for getting the word out about their business. One client sent me her notes on her self-help topic for women. Working closely with her, I compiled her notes into a 12-page eBook format, which she initially sold as a $27 download. After some time, she decided she wanted to upgrade the product. We extrapolated the existing content into an interactive 40-page workbook providing note space. She sold the workbook on her website as a download for $47.

One of my favorite things about an eBook is that it is delivered electronically. You could incorporate a few videos with your eBook and increase the monetary charge for this product. You could interview leading experts in your field and incorporate that into the product. This all ties in to the value of your services! Your one eBook and other accompanying products just went from a $15 eBook download to a $97 product bundle by incorporating some videos and interviews. If you sold 100 copies of the eBook download, your profit would be $1,500; if you sold 50 of the $97 product bundle, your profit would be $4,850. I think this demonstrates the power of information products.

Tele-Classes

A tele-course or tele-class or tele-seminar all refer to people connecting via phone. The idea behind a tele-class or tele-seminar is that you are utilizing a one-to-many approach in your teaching. Rather than preparing material for a one-to-one delivery, a tele-delivery program allows you to be on the phone with many participants at once.

Think of a tele-class as a workshop you conduct by phone. The participants dial into a bridge line where everyone is connected and the workshop takes place. There are many services available to host such calls and many are free, such as FreeConferenceCall.com® or FreeConference.com®. Some services offer additional features including screen sharing, so you can show a PowerPoint® presentation. There are even services available to host international callers.

Tele-classes are a great way to stay in touch with the people who are on your marketing list. You could host a monthly tele-class and talk about *10 Tips to Success in Public Speaking* or *Five Hot Ways to Dress on a First Date,* for example. The idea here is you could make tele-classes an ongoing, monthly subscription service. You could also incorporate a closed Facebook® group for members only so that the participants have another avenue to interface with you and with each other—all building camaraderie and rapport—thus leading to more value that you have provided.

Webinars

A webinar is a web-based seminar. Typically, a seminar or workshop or presentation is presented via the Internet. Many service providers for webinars also offer a recording feature that can be utilized after the event is over. A webinar is a great way to literally get in front of your prospects or clients and host a presentation with interaction as if you were in the same room.

There are a wide variety of webinar hosting services available free and many charge nominal fees, such as Any Meeting® or GoToMeeting®. I am currently working with a client who is rolling out a webinar series for which he plans to get 1,000 or more subscribers on a regular $17/month subscription: $1,000 x 17 = $17,000/month from one information product!

A webinar can be constructed from the live workshops you have created and want to take to a web format. After you conduct the webinar, you can then create a product that you sell on your website as a downloadable. You could include a workbook that goes along with the webinar that the participant will work through as they watch the webinar. Like with the tele-classes, webinars can become a subscription-based series that you are doing on a regular basis.

Podcasts

A podcast is a unique type of digital media that can become part of a series, in a video or audio format that can be subscribed to and downloaded from your website. The word "podcast" comes from the term "broadcast" and from the iPod® to create "podcast." Although a podcast can be listened to in a variety of ways including on your computer, many are listened to via portable media players such as an iPod® or MP3 player. Content for a podcast can be short tips and ideas for your followers or subscribers or you can have longer content, such as interviews or a radio show format.

There are varying degrees of involvement for podcasts—you can create your own website and files, edit them and post them, or you can utilize a third-party service to host, such as BlogTalkRadio®. In setting up a channel on BlogTalkRadio, decide the format you are going to use to host your show, considering whether it will be only you each time or if you will host guests on your show. Alternatively, you could reach out to various shows and see if they are looking for guest experts. There is a free service available at RadioGuestList.com® where you can sign up to receive daily emails to get radio interviews, talk show expert publicity, podcast guest and sponsors.

Videos

Tying in with podcasts, videos are another way to reach your target market. In my opinion, videos are highly under-utilized and a very effective way to reach your prospects. A client I worked with recently did a five part series on financial freedom. She created each video with her web cam and we uploaded them onto YouTube®. We then embedded them onto her website—now she can refer her clients to visit her website and get her five tips for financial freedom. She can also promote her website link throughout social media and be able to drive traffic back to her website, get more sign ups, have more people viewing her videos, sharing her videos and wanting to sign up with her for other services. Videos are an effective way to interact with your audience and can be done and uploaded in a few minutes at your computer.

Plan your content as you did with your articles and prepare a video for each of your "Ten Steps to XYZ." Spend three to five minutes on each video to maintain engagement with your audience.

Food for Thought

Information products are a great way to add additional streams of income to your business. Articles can be proliferated by article directory sites that are picked up on various websites. This may get you an interview on a radio or television show.

Information products add to your existing product base or allow you to create products to begin building your online store. In large part, the cost of creating information products is only that of your time as all formats are digital, and there is no need for printing your workbooks or burning CDs or DVDs.

You may need to hire professionals in order to help support you in getting your content up onto your website or hire a virtual assistant who will help get your articles onto the article directories. These costs incurred will help free up your time to be in the field, meeting new clients and bringing in more business. Another tidbit for your information product success: once you create these products, they are always available to sell on your website, offer to prospects at a speaking engagement and much more.

"Action is the foundational key to all success."
–Pablo Picasso, Spanish artist

Resources

• Article Directory sites		www.searcharticles.net www.ezinearticles.com www.articlesbase.com
• Webinars	*GoToMeeting* *AnyMeeting*	www.gotomeeting.com/fec www.anymeeting.com
• Videos	*YouTube*	www.youtube.com
• Podcasts	*BlogTalkRadio*	www.blogtalkradio.com
• Tele-Classes	*FreeConferenceCall* *FreeConference*	www.freeconferencecall.com www.freeconference.com
• PodCasts	*RadioGuestList*	www.radioguestlist.com radiotalk-show-guests.html

With the call to action and the resources list above, you now have all the tools you need to create profitable information products today. I would love to hear what is working for you and what is helping you grow your business.

Get in Action!

I encourage you to pick at least three of the information products above and get in action today to create them and begin marketing them on your website.

Dortha Hise

Your success is my business!

(916) 817-6878
dortha@dorthahise.com
www.dorthahise.com

Dortha Hise is passionate about helping others be successful. Born and raised in California, she began her first business at the age of 11 breeding hamsters and selling the offspring to local pet stores. She graduated from Loyola University of Chicago with a bachelor of arts in psychology in 1998 and received a bachelor of science in criminal justice in 2003 from the University of Nevada, Las Vegas.

A serial entrepreneur, Dortha runs a successful virtual consulting business and a web design and development business. She offers a variety of support to her clients from research and phone calls to web design and social media support.

An ardent advocate for breast cancer cure, Dortha has walked in the Sacramento American Cancer Society Making Strides® walk since 2006. In 2010, after losing a close friend to breast cancer, Dortha raised more than $2,000 and walked 40 miles in the Avon Walk for Breast Cancer®. Dortha and her best friend and husband, Jason, have coordinated medical screening clinics to benefit the Shriners Hospital for Children® and currently oversee all the screening clinics in Northern California.

Set the Stage for Your Speaking Success

By Elizabeth Bachman

I am rocking my speech—in the zone, confident, positive, smiling. Every line—practiced for days—comes out of my mouth as if I just thought of it, and it's the perfect thing to say, with perfect timing, tone and gestures. I crack a joke, and the audience laughs. I can feel the flow of energy from me to them and the flow from them to me. It's as if I am a channel for my message. All the time I spent getting the words just right, practicing my gestures and where to stand on stage—all that time mastering my craft—is paying off. My techniques are automatic, and I am free to just stand before my people and communicate. I say my last line and they leap to their feet in a standing ovation. As I step off the stage, the crowd is waiting for me, and they all want to buy....

Sounds fabulous, doesn't it?

Speaking in public is one of the fastest ways to promote your business or practice. It can be an essential part of your marketing plan. Instead of talking to people one on one to persuade them to sign up with you, you have an entire room full of potential clients.

Whether you are talking to your boss or speaking to a crowd, public speaking is like putting on a show. It is all theatre—in the best possible way. If you do it right, your ideal clients will come running up, begging to work with you.

Do Not Be a Talking Head, Be a Rock Star!

There is much more to fabulous speaking than just standing in front of a group, talking about what you do. We have all seen the dreaded "talking heads" who read from their script in a monotone, or worse, project a slide and then read every word to you. Yawn.

When you are in front of a group presenting an idea or offering a product, how you speak is more important than what you say. Only 7 percent of what people perceive about you comes from your words. The other 93 percent comes from nonverbal cues such as how you look and how you deliver your message. Is your mouth saying one thing and your body language another? Are you nervous and betraying it? Are you so involved in what you have to offer that you forget to take the audience into account?

"Public speaking" is actually a misnomer. The great presenters are connectors, performers and communicators. In short, they are rock stars.

There are hundreds of ways to become a rock star presenter. Let's concentrate on the three Ps: perception, presence and projection.

The world of the theatre is all about these principles. I was a stage-struck kid, with dreams of becoming a great actress. As I grew older, I found that directing was more fun. From acting and directing in theatre, I soon made my way to opera, and there I found my home. My great passions in life are music, theatre, languages and travel. Opera has them all.

My career as an opera director has taken me around the world, and I loved every minute of it. I learned about perception, presence and projection by working in opera companies large and small. Whether I am working with speakers or directing such legendary performers as Luciano Pavarotti, these same principles apply.

Perception

You may have heard about the three main learning styles—visual, auditory and kinesthetic. Visual learners learn best when they see something. Auditory learners really need to hear it, say it again and hear it come out of their mouths. The kinesthetics do not really get it until they have walked through something or taken it apart to see how it works. In public speaking, you want to appeal to all three.

The challenge is this: It is all too easy to only use your learning style. This means that you are leaving money on the table because you are missing the others. You need to mix it up!

You only have eight minutes before your audience needs a change of pace. Use flip charts, whiteboards or slides for the visual learners. For the auditory types, find exercises where the audience must say something or speak with a neighbor. They will learn better if they hear the words coming out of their mouths. Have people write things down or fill in blanks. This kinesthetic technique accelerates the learning process.

Once you know this, you can go through your presentation and find organic ways to augment it. This may sound obvious, but you would be amazed how often experienced speakers forget to do this.

It is all too easy to use your own chief learning style for the whole presentation and then wonder why some members of the audience are glazing over.

My client Adam is a business consultant for entrepreneurs. As an auditory learner, he learns best by listening to podcasts. He felt silly using flip charts, so he would spend most of his presentations talking about his tracking systems. The only visual aid he had was a handout with charts and graphs.

Adam could not figure out why his talks did not bring in more clients. Then one day he noticed a woman in the third row with a pack of mints, arranging them in patterns on the table. He was instantly thrown back to his student days. He had an incredibly boring professor, and the only thing that kept him awake was to bring a pack of five-flavor Lifesavers® and spend the hour creating different arrangements and orders of eating.

Adam came to me for help, and we went through his presentation. We found places where he could write on the whiteboard to attract the visual learners and use exercises to help the kinesthetics. His ideal clients were entrepreneurs who did not think in numbers, so we kept his charts and graphs and gave him narratives and metaphors for each one. We decided that if he used slides, it would be too easy to revert to a lecturing style. The need to be more kinesthetic applied to him too.

Once he started speaking to all the learning styles, his sales improved, and he found that he loved performing. The more he did it, the more he discovered parts of himself that had been suppressed. That made him an even better presenter. The woman with the candy never came back, but he thanks her for the wake-up call.

Perception means paying attention to *all* the ways you want to be perceived.

Presence

Everyone has a different definition of "stage presence," and we can all agree that we know it when we see it. When the presenter is grounded, confident and knowledgeable, we want to hear what they have to say and learn from them. As an audience, we know a lot. We know when someone is faking it, when they do not think they will succeed, when they are questioning the sanity of standing up and asking us to believe them.

The key is to stand in your power and believe that you deserve the audience's attention, respect and support. In short, to *be fabulous.*

The definition of fabulous is to be worthy of having fables told about you.

Everyone's "fabulous" is different. It can be being bright and shiny, or it can be classy and elegant or it can be deeply rooted in the earth and connected to the universe. Think of all the fables about Mother Earth. My goal is not to turn you into a flash, fakey actor-type, but to help you find out what makes you YOU. Finding your unique voice will allow you to be fabulous in whichever way works for you.

I learned this the hard way.

In addition to directing operas, as the years went on, I began teaching more and more, passing on the things I learned to the next generation. In 2005, I founded the Tyrolean Opera Program (TOP Opera), a summer opera training program in the Austrian Alps. Spending the summer making music in the mountains was going to be wonderful.

The problem was money. I had to raise $100,000 to produce the program. I dreaded it. For the first time in my life, I had to make speeches on my own behalf. I had to ask people to write a check to support my dream.

I was terrified, and at first, I was terrible.

During those first speeches, I forgot everything I had ever known or taught. Whether stage fright or a loss of confidence, the audience knew I was not sure of my own value.

No wonder nobody donated that first time!

What saved me—as it has saved many an actor, singer and presenter—was coaching. A smart friend came to one of my speeches and told me, "Did you know that when you ask for money, your face gets all gray? Worse, you look afraid and desperate."

I realized that I had lost my stage presence. I stopped being grounded. My friend would be a great audience. I could not fix my presentation without having someone reflect it back to me. She would tell me exactly what would work with just the right balance of criticism and love. As a director, for years, I had coached actors and singers. Now I needed one myself.

The more I practiced, with the tricks my coach taught me, the better I got. The better I got, the more donations came in. TOP Opera became a reality, and then I finally got the real payoff. At the end of the first season, a student hugged me and said, "You have changed my life!"

The lesson for me was to stand in my power and connect to being fabulous.

Imagine yourself onstage in front of a group of clients. Do you think your audience members are thinking terrible things about you? Are your inner gremlins having a field day telling you that they hate you, and so on?

Stop!

Once you start thinking of the audience as hostile, you begin broadcasting your insecurity. The truth is, you cannot actually know what is in your listeners' heads. They want you to be wonderful. They have taken the time to come hear you because they are hoping that you have a solution to their problems. If you are stuck in your own head, at the mercy of your inner gremlins, you cut off any chance of actually communicating.

Go back to your imaginary group, and imagine that this room is your room, and that they are all guests at your party. Greet them with joy, knowing that they have come because they really want to be there with you. As you stand there, feel your connection to the earth and feel the strength and power that is coursing up through you. Know that you deserve to be in front of your friends because the service or product that you offer will truly help them.

You will not become unflappable overnight, of course. The key is to practice, so that when you realize that you are off track, you can ground yourself again. You can get back to your own party, and welcome everyone else to join it.

Project Your Passion

If you are grounded and standing in your power you will be interesting on stage, but you will not necessarily sell anything. Adding projection means including your audience in your presentation, by understanding what they want.

It is a duet.

Project yourself into their shoes. What do they really want from your presentation? Most of us spend so much time talking about what we do that we forget to talk about the benefits to the client. Your clients do not want to know how you do something; they want to know whether you can fix their accounting systems or make their migraines go away.

Do not focus on what you think they need, but what they want. Address the urgent problem that brought them there and show them that you have the perfect answer. Once they begin working with you, you can give them what they actually need.

What nonverbal messages are you projecting? When people in an audience feel comfortable, they are more willing to buy. Are you projecting anxiety, or are you inviting them to your party and sharing your passion for what you offer?

When working on your presence and projection, it is very important to get help from someone else. Practicing in the mirror is not enough. Your reflection will not give you an independent and objective reaction.

Offering independent and objective reactions is what directors—whether of opera, theatre or movies—do. A director does not go on stage—she watches and evaluates the performer, looking for what is unique, and bringing it out in the most effective way. When you see Tom Hanks or Meryl Streep on screen, they are not working alone. They have worked with a director to shape their performance.

Learning how to speak effectively in public is a process. Here is a great way to get started.

Go back to your imaginary audience of party guests and spread your arms as if you are giving them a big hug. Feel your fabulous energy and let it expand to fill the whole room, so that all your party guests share your energy. They are ready to listen, ready to learn, ready to be inspired by your passion for what you are offering. The more they are inspired, the more their energy comes back to you – and, in turn, lifts you higher.

Now, they are in your space as a part of your fabulous energy. Becoming part of your energy is the connection that will bring people in the audience running up to work with you.

The secrets of perception, presence and projection all work together.

- **Perception**, on your part, means paying attention to the message you are sending, both verbal and nonverbal. It means using all the styles of learning to convey your message. If you do not employ all the learning styles during your presentation, you will only be truly communicating with members of the audience who perceive the world the same way you do. The other two-thirds will walk away with their money still in their pocket because you did not reach them on their terms.
- **Presence** means thinking of your audience as your guests. This is one of the ways to have great stage presence: Stand in your power and feel totally at home in front of a group. Audiences can tell when we are ungrounded. Standing in your power will make you feel fabulous and make you a better speaker.
- **Projecting** your passion means expanding your presence to include the audience or prospective clients and customers. What do your ideal clients want? How can you design your speech to provide solutions to their problems? When you are in front of your people, you must connect to your power, and then project that feeling of comfort and confidence to include them.

Perception, presence and projection are three of the most important secrets to speaking with power and confidence, truly communicating with your people in the most effective way and closing more sales!

If you are passionate about your product or service, if you truly believe that your clients benefit from working with you, then communicating that passion live and in person will reach your ideal clients on many more levels than they will get from a video, a webpage or a flyer. Remember, you cannot see yourself when you are speaking. So whether it is me or someone else, find a coach to work with. Your people deserve all of your fabulousness.

To paraphrase Mark Twain, the difference between a talking head and a rock star is like the difference between the lightning bug and the lightning.

You are fabulous.

Be the lightning!

Elizabeth Bachman

Be Fabulous
Wow Your Audience
Beyond Mere Words
(415) 967-1014
Fabtraining1@gmail.com
www.befabuloustraining.com

Elizabeth Bachman is passionate about helping people shine onstage. Using her thirty years of experience as an international opera director, she works with speakers, authors and business professionals to find their unique voice, stand in their power, and truly communicate with their audiences. In short, to be fabulous!

In workshops, webinars and solo coaching, Elizabeth's clients learn the secret to owning the stage, techniques to make stage fright work for you, and how to ignite the audience to take action so that they beg to work with you. Whether working with a client to jazz up her act, punch up his pitch or polish a presentation, Elizabeth helps her clients stop procrastinating, get past their emotional blocks and take their show on the road.

Elizabeth has directed more than fifty operas in more than thirty opera companies in the United States, Argentina and Japan. Fluent in five languages, she has directed such legendary artists as Luciano Pavarotti. She is also the founder and artistic director of the Tyrolean Opera Program (TOP Opera), a summer opera training program in the Austrian Alps.

Using Facebook® to Build Your Business

By April P. Cooper

In 2009, I started a personal Facebook® page. To my surprise, many people were on Facebook already. I started to add friends and family, and my contacts grew from 25 to 252! Then in early 2010, I started to learn about having a business page, which I started. My connections took off because I was watching and studying the time people were on Facebook and the content posted.

Through my connections on Facebook, people began inviting me to their business events and mixers. This is where the high tech became high touch. I would travel to events from five to one-hundred miles away, depending on the people that were going to be there. My friends list started to increase. This networking thing was working! I now have many referral buddies who have shared my information with others, and I do the same for them.

A question people ask all the time is, "How can I use Facebook to build my business?" I explain that there are many ways to expand business on the Internet with Facebook. For example, you can search for people whom you want to know, based on their business and whether they might be a good fit as a partner or for a joint venture. This is also a good way for you to become known. Since you are connecting with the people you have chosen, when you come to know, like and trust them, they will do the same for you. They will share your name with others via what I call free advertising.

Let's find out how you can use Facebook to build your business. I will start with some concepts you need to know.

Pages

- "Personal Pages" represent individuals and must be held under an individual name.
- "Fan Pages" allow an organization, business, celebrity or other entity to maintain a professional presence on Facebook. You may only create Fan Pages for real organizations of which you are an authorized representative.
- Pages are managed by admins who have personal Facebook profiles called "timelines."
- Your "timeline" is your collection of top photos, stories and life events. These are some of the things you can do on your timeline.
- Pages are not separate Facebook accounts and do not have separate login information from your timeline.
- People who choose to connect to—"Like"—your page will be able to see that you are the page owner and can see more ways to connect with you on your personal page from just one location.

Signing Up for Facebook

To set up a personal page, go to the sign-up page, just provide your full name, email address, desired password, gender and date of birth.

After you complete the sign-up form, check your email address that you provided to set up your account for a message from Facebook asking you to confirm the account. This ensures no one else uses your email to set up an account without your permission. Clicking on the confirmation link will complete the sign up process.

To set up a Facebook Fan Page, go to Facebook.com:

- Beneath the sign-up information, click on the link with the words "Create a Page."
- In the top right corner, login to your account.
- Pick which category your business is under.
- Fill in company name and other information requested.
- Put a check mark in the box with the words, "I agree to Facebook page terms."
- Click on the blue box that reads "Get Started."
- On the next page, start to upload a picture, type in your business information, such as address, email and website. Your phone number is optional.
- Now, start posting!

How do you expect to expand your business without using social media? Having a Fan Page is like an extension of your personal page. When anyone meets you in person these days, many ask if you have a Facebook account. If your answer is "yes," the next step will be an investigation. This is what I do if I am going to do business with someone or I want to refer them. I check out their wall of comments and their friends. I also click on their employment to see information about their business. You can also search for their email and website addresses. Facebook, by itself, can take you further than you wanted to go. The point is to stay focused and look for information about the person and his or her business.

This is why having a Facebook Fan Page is important—you want people who could be potential clients, joint venture partners, or referral buddies to be able to connect with you easily and effortlessly. Facebook Fan Pages let you do this.

Secret Hint: Remember to add your business Fan Page to your profile employment on your personal page so that the employment profile links back to your Fan Page. This keeps the connection to you instead of away from you to someone else.

Network Using Facebook

When networking using Facebook, you want to search networking groups you can join. Some are free and open to everyone. Some are a closed group and you have to ask to join or be recommended by someone in the group. Being a part of these groups can help move your business forward. The groups you want to search out are those that have two benefits. One, choose a group that has mixers so you can meet one another in person. Second, choose a group that is providing valuable information, both online and in person.

There are plenty of groups on Facebook that have Fan Pages. For example:

- Women's networking groups
- Business-to-business networking groups
- Mom entrepreneurial networking groups
- Successful thinkers networking mixer groups

Secret Hint: Search for groups where you might find your ideal client or potential referral buddies.

Set Yourself Apart Using Facebook

If you are in direct sales, your company gives you a system to follow that you cannot wavier from. There are action steps you can take that will not jeopardize you with your company or upline.

Your company wants you to follow their system because they believe you will be successful in their business if you do. In addition, some companies have a social media platform that they want you to use. However, you need to set yourself apart from your colleagues if you want people to notice you as a representative for the company.

You can brand yourself by using the information on your company's Fan Page on your own Fan Page with your personal experience added to it. You also want to have plenty of pictures of you at events, receiving awards, with top producers in the company, and with you in front of the room speaking. This shows you as a leader who educates and teaches your team how to succeed. People want to see this information if they are going to connect with you. Have your past clients, customers and friends who have bought from you post testimonials on your Fan Page stating what they have purchased from you. If you are allowed, have the logo of the company on your Fan Page and post photos of products with you in the picture. You also can have video and pictures at events. Just be aware and read the rules you have to follow when it comes to advertising on social media.

If you are an entrepreneur or have a small business or storefront, you have more leeway when it comes to using Facebook for your business, because you control what you want to post on your Fan Page wall. The logo is yours, and you can brand your business easier.

Just as for direct sales companies, you want lots of pictures, rewards and any other information that shows you are an expert at your craft.

For example, if you own a restaurant and were voted best in your community, you want to show that. Your bottom line is getting fans to connect with you to come into your store or request service from you.

Secret Hint: Make your presence on Facebook *about you,* not just *by you.*

The Best Time To Be on Facebook

As a business owner and expert on using Facebook to build a business, I studied the best times to post on Facebook. I recommend you post at least three to four times a day and about three days a week Monday through Thursday. The best times of the day to post are:

8:45 a.m. – 9:15 a.m.
11:45 a.m. – 1:15 p.m.
4:45 p.m. – 5:30 p.m.
8:30 p.m. – 9:30 p.m.

More people are on Facebook during these times. The morning is a good time to catch people like the stay-at-home moms after they have dropped off kids at school, people just getting into work and those who showed up for work earlier and are taking a break. Lunch is always a good time, and the last two times will capture people who are getting ready to leave work, who have finished dinner or just before bed.

On Friday and Saturday, post the events that are fun and exciting and include video and pictures. This shows you are not all about business and you do enjoy family, friends and fun.

Secret Hint: Use the time for your target market, not for you.

What to Post on Facebook as a Business Owner

As I mentioned above, Monday through Thursday are days when you want to talk about tips about your product and services that can benefit the public. You want to have some before and after pictures, the do's and don'ts, the ups and downs, and especially solutions to help your reading audience. This makes you more trustworthy since you are not posting just the good things about your product and services. If anyone is going to buy or use your service, they can rely on you to be truthful and honest with them, and will probably purchase from you. This is what you want.

For example, if you are a caterer and have pictures of events, post them to show your audience what a properly catered event would look like, as well as what to look out for when hiring a caterer for an event. In this case, you are using photos to explain the do's and don'ts.

Secret Hint: Facebook fans and friends need to get to know you in order to trust you.

Quick Tips

You can hire a virtual personal assistant (VPA) to do it all for you. If you do, I suggest you learn Facebook basics so you have an idea of what is going on.

Where to go for Facebook coaching basics:

- Use the free help center on Facebook to get answers to any questions you have about Facebook, or
- For one-on-one, step-by-step coaching basics on Facebook, make an appointment with a VPA.

Where to go for a custom Facebook Fan Page if you want video, opt-in form, banners, and surveys.

- Go to www.facebook.com/sociallynow

Where to go if you do not have time to do it all yourself, yet still want to have a presence on Facebook.

1. Go to www.ExecutiveVPA.com and register your name and email address, or

2. Send an email to executivevpa@gmail.com

Facebook Lingo—Fan Pages

- **Likes.** You want people to "like" your Fan Page by clicking the "Like" button. When you click **Like** on a Facebook Page, in an advertisement or on content apart from Facebook, you are making a connection—and you want connections to be made! When people "like" your page, it will appear on their wall or timeline, and it may appear in their News Feed.

  Facebook Pages you "like" may post updates to your News Feed or send you messages.

- **Q & A section.** This is where you post questions that might come up from clients or fans for others to see. You can post a poll question on your page asking fans what they want to know about your services or for the best suggestions for your business. The answers can come from you or your fans.

Facebook Lingo—Facebook-Personal Page

- **Friends.** You add them, or they add you. You are limited to a maximum of 5,000.
- **Subscribers.** These are people waiting to be added as your friend, people you do not want on your friends list who can still get updates from your page, or people you are interested in who are not friends. Even if they have 5,000 friends, they can subscribe to you. This allows you to keep up with journalists, celebrities, political figures and other people you are interested in who have 5,000-plus friends. You can get their public updates in your News Feed by going to their profile and clicking on the Subscribe button. Once they subscribe, they can see your public posts in their News Feed.
- **Subscriptions.** These are people in whom you have an interest in and with whom you want to be friends, yet cannot because they have the maximum of 5,000 friends. They show up in your subscriptions tab on the left of your personal page.

Do not let Facebook overwhelm you— it is very simple to do yourself, get help from a social media expert or have a virtual assistant do it for you. The key is to just do it so your business can be exposed to others all over the Facebook network. This can increase revenue and grow your business.

This is your mission—if you choose to take it.

April P. Cooper

Executive VPA

Let Me Be the Time You Don't Have to Market Your Business

(209) 915-7219

executivevpa@gmail.com

www.executivevpa.com

April P. Cooper is a woman child of God, a wife, a mother of five, an entrepreneur consultant, a business owner, an author, an educator and a public speaker. She has been in the network marketing business since the 1990s and has helped many team members achieve high levels. She guides her team in the right direction with a proven system. She is now an Internet marketing business coach and consultant who helps her clients' businesses increase revenue.

April has always dedicated her life to striving for the betterment of the people she loves. Her goal is to enhance the lives of women by teaching them the best way to brand themselves with social media as a platform and to move their businesses forward. April helps her clients with branding that sets them apart from competitors by giving them a social media presence, and teaching them to give value and showing them how to stand out at a business networking event.

A resident of Stockton, California, April has a bachelor of arts in education from the University of The Pacific and masters of business administration from American InterContinental University.

■ ■ ■

Using Blogs and Video to Build Your Business

Get Your Name Out There in a Big Way and Increase Profits!

By Robin O'Neal Smith, MEd, ITS

In today's economy, everyone wants to be successful in his or her business. It is more important than ever before to become noticed and put your best foot forward, so you can be competitive with larger companies in the global marketplace. Entrepreneurs can do this with social media, specifically blogging and video.

Why is social media important? Social media is not going away. It is only in its infancy and will continue to grow for years. Which company or business would you purchase something from? The business you have never had a relationship with or the company that has engaged in conversation with you and has given you free ideas and "how-to" videos? I know which one I would want to do business with—and I bet you do, too.

People want to purchase from and work with people they know and trust, not a company or someone they do not know. It is all about relationships! You want to have a relationship with your customers. Blogs are a form of social media and they most certainly help you to build a relationship with your target market.

What Is Your Business and Why Do You Need a Blog?

Social media can help your business to grow and become more profitable, regardless of the business you own. Social media done right can help every business, from hair salons to funeral homes, from greenhouses to information products, from petroleum companies to small gift shops, from art galleries to chiropractors and from organizers to party planners. I cannot think of any businesses that could not grow with the help of social media.

You hear talk of social media everywhere—about business owners trying to learn how to use it. The best way for you to get started with social media is to create a blog and post to it on a regular basis. Blogs are a way of interacting with customers and building an ongoing relationship. Include some video that explains your business and/or some "how to" videos for the products you provide.

You might be asking yourself, "I already have a web page. Isn't that enough?" However, a static web page is not always enough. While a blog can be part of your website, a blog is different from a standard website. A blog is published in a chronological fashion, and the content is updated regularly. Readers can interact and leave comments, and they can receive the information via email signup or Real Simple Syndication (RSS) feed. RSS can also be referred to as Rich Site Summary and is a format for delivering regularly changing web content. You can also connect to Facebook®, Twitter®, LinkedIn®, Google+® and other social networks and post about your blog to help you drive traffic to it.

How Can a Blog Increase Your Online Visibility?

Think of blogging as a "gathering place" for your customers where they can find out about new products, services and discounts, or can pass on information to and from others about your niche. Making your blog available so people can sign up to get your posts will remind them to come back. Posting to your blog adds value to your customer's day.

When you start making posts, customers will read them and make comments, ask questions or click "Like." When people make comments, you want to respond and engage them. Ask questions and let them know you value their opinion.

If some only read your posts and others' comments, they are still engaged with you. While there may be times when you think no one is reading, someone will see you in person or purchase something and mention they learned about it from your blog post. Sometimes, it takes a while to see results.

What Blogging Platform Should You Use?

You have a choice of several blogging platforms. I have used several and will give you some information about each.

Blogger at www.blogger.com is part of the Google® family. It is free and very easy to use. Simple word processing is all that is needed. However, you have limited flexibility in how the end user views the blog. It is housed on the Blogger® website, and all blog addresses created here have the domain ending of "blogspot.com." This would be my first choice for a super simple, easy-to-use product when customization is not important.

WordPress® has two products. WordPress.com is very similar to Blogger. It is housed on the WordPress site and the domain ends in wordpress.com. It is also free and easy to use. It provides more advanced options than Blogger and requires little more than word processing skills.

You could begin using one of these very quickly to get your blog started. I do not recommend them for long-term use because each platform owns their site and the content. It is sort of like being a digital sharecropper, building your business on someone else's land. They own your page and your information. They have various rules and, for any reason, can close you down, lose your content, or start charging. You are at their mercy, and all of your hard work could be lost.

The third option is also through WordPress, using *www.wordpress.org*. It is also *free*. The difference is it is housed *on your site*. You can house it on your web page or another site you purchase for hosting. You put it under your domain, so your blog address would not include "blogspot" or "wordpress" as part of the domain. You can use this option to build your entire website!

You can also purchase excellent step-by-step instructions and video of "how to" do-it-yourself from several sources such as The Social Networking Academy (www.thesocialnetworkingacademy.com), Revenue Recharge (www.revenuerecharge.com), Michelle Shaeffer (www.michelleshaeffer.com) and on my site, Be Social, Get Success (www.besocialgetsuccess.com).

You can build a website and blog on other sites. However, these are the three most popular for business.

What Should You Blog About?

So, you decide you want a blog. What will you blog about? This is a question many people ask. First, do not feel compelled to post to your blog every day. Start by committing to once a week. When that becomes routine, you increase to twice a week.

- Are there any holidays you can tie to your business?
- What is going on with your business? Are you running any special sales or seasonal events that you can write about?
- What about your customers? How can you help them with a problem? How can your products solve their dilemma?
- Can you feature a special customer?
- Are there any new information and products customers need to know about?
- Can you do a "how-to" video featuring current products?

Take a piece of paper and write down every possible idea you can write about during the upcoming month. Then plan your posts in the order you think you want to publish them. Most people find they have many more topics than they have time to write about. Perhaps some can be used for next month. Once you get comfortable with this, you can plan months in advance. Just take a calendar and make it your blogging calendar. Write down the titles of planned posts.

Tips for Successful Blogging

The following tips will help you to create successful blog posts that will keep your readers coming back for more.

- **Keep it simple.** Life is complicated enough, so make things as easy as possible for them.
- **Keep it short.** A couple of paragraphs will ensure your readers have time to read your posts. The longer the post, the fewer people will read.

- **Make the content relevant.** You want readers to find your information helpful and informative.
- **Be funny.** Not all the time, but occasionally. Humor sells.
- **Show your passion!** You need to love what you are writing about and why it is important. When people feel your passion, they engage.
- **Pay attention to your title.** Is it catchy and backed up by content?
- **Tell a story.** Weave tidbits about your life and business into your blog, and do not make the blog about you. It is about what the customer wants.
- **Be consistent.** Do not give your readers ten posts one week and none the next. Give them consistency on an ongoing basis. If you have the time to write ten posts, schedule them in advance for the next ten weeks or two per week for the next five weeks.
- **Use pictures or video.** Keep your audience guessing as to what will be on your blog next. To add interest and increase engagement, try adding pictures or video.

Using Video to Increase Enthusiasm for Your Business

Not only is video the best form of communication, it is also a way to personally connect with each and every one of your readers to build a relationship. Remember, people do business with people who they know, like and trust. By being able to see you and experience your personality, viewers are much more likely to feel like they know you. A feeling of trust creates a priceless relationship.

Videos are personal. Using video with your own image also gives your potential clients an easier way to get to know you. It brings out your voice and your facial expressions, creating a much stronger way to interact with visitors.

Eye contact, even in video, gives you an advantage over those who are not doing it. Video differentiates you from everyone else.

Video allows you to show and tell about your product or skill. Video demonstrations and explanations of concepts are often much easier to understand than the written word.

Given the immense popularity of online video sites, video could be used to tap into different marketing channels and new opportunities. When you use both text and video, you are reaching a wider audience than you would reach with text alone.

Tips for Creating Videos

Video blogging is easy to do because virtually any camera, any room and any lighting will work.

Before you get in front of the lens, consider these tips:

- Do not be afraid to be yourself. Allow your personality to show through and do not stress over perfection because little mistakes make you human.
- Wear clothes that fit your body. A little too snug is better than baggy. The camera adds ten pounds and shapeless apparel will make you look heavier and less polished on camera.
- Make sure clothing is comfortable when you are sitting or standing. Make sure your clothes look good in both positions.
- Solid-colored clothes are best. Make sure your clothes do not blend in with the background. You want to stand out, yet not be too bold or clashing. Excellent colors are blue (any shade), tan, medium tones and pastels, purple, lavender, wine, burgundy and gray.
- Avoid wearing black, white or red on television or video. Even the best cameras have trouble with these colors.
- Do not wear clothing with tight or large patterns, geometric shapes or pinstripes, which cause an optical illusion and take the focus away from what you are presenting.

- Make sure your makeup, wardrobe and hair are consistent with your message. A professional does not look like he just rolled out of bed.
- If you are doing a full-length video, wear shoes that look new.
- Wear all-season clothing since the video is aired and viewed year-round.
- Avoid flashy or jangly jewelry that reflects light and makes noise that will be noticeable. Simple accessories are best.
- Add a call to action. What do you want the viewer to do?
- Make sure you have copyright permission to use music, graphics and so on.
- Use built-in royalty-free material in the video editor.
- Do not make a commercial. It needs to have content. Plan it. YouTube® has a policy against commercials.

Where Can Videos Be Posted?

The number of video-sharing sites has increased in recent years. Some are very popular and allow editing as well. You may have heard of Google Video®, Vimeo® and JumpCut®. The most popular and best place to get traffic is YouTube.

YouTube is currently the second largest search engine in the world. The average time a person spends on YouTube continues to increase. Most people watch two to four videos once they reach the YouTube site.

"A good video can make all the difference."
—Brian May, English musician

How to Include Video in Your Blog

Once you have your video posted to YouTube, you can then put a link to it in your blog, or better yet, embed the video code in your blog, so your readers can click and watch the video right on your site.

Video is easy to embed. Once the video is created on YouTube, you click on the "Share" button, and YouTube gives you a choice to link information or embed information. Click on the embed information and copy it. Paste it into the HTML code of your blog, and you are ready to share your video.

Some Tips for Using Video in Your Blog

You want to use video to enhance your blog and increase interest. To do that, you need to follow a few simple tips.

- Always allow your visitors to decide whether to click a link to view the video or not. Video streamed automatically when visitors land on the page can be jarring and result in site avoidance.
- Most visitors will view your media streams from office desktops, so audio needs to be clear and unobtrusive. This means you should avoid including large spontaneous crashes, beeps, sirens, screams and so on.
- Keep it short. A two- to eight-minute video is long enough. If you really want to get your message across, keep it as short as possible.
- Focus on unique content, not your product. Offer a video with educational or inspiring content related to your niche that a viewer cannot get elsewhere. Giving viewers a positive takeaway will help them to remember you in the future. That lasting impression is far more valuable than trying to get a quick sell.
- You should create at least one call to action in your video, where you tell people exactly what you want them to do next and why. For example, "Go to www.yourcompanyname.com to grab Part 2 of this video—and hurry! You can only get it free till Thursday!"
- Encourage comments. Remember, controversial, funny and unusual videos build readership. The more people talk about your video, the more your visitors will return to your page to see what is new in the discussion.

Use Social Media and Drive Traffic to Your Blog and Video

Do not assume that because you posted a blog or video online, people will be able to find it. You will need to promote it. One way to do that is to post a link on your other social media site pages, like Twitter, Facebook, LinkedIn and StumbleUpon®.

You can encourage readers/viewers to re-tweet, share and forward the information. If you have joint venture partners or others in a group, you can ask them to share with their readers as well.

Blogging and using video can help you to engage your audience, grow your business, pre-sell products, demonstrate products, teach your customers, drive traffic to your sites and grow your mailing list. All of these will help you to increase profits. Just a little time can reap big rewards. Start blogging and using video today—you will be amazed at what they can do for you and your business.

Robin O'Neal Smith, MEd, ITS

Be Social, Get Success

Inspiring Online Success and Profits!

(814) 502-6318

robin@besocialgetsuccess.com

www.besocialgetsuccess.com

After twenty years in the educational field as a teacher, technology integration specialist and director of technology, Robin O'Neal Smith found her true passion where technology intersects with social media. Passionate about social networking, she founded the social media company, Be Social, Get Success, to teach people how to use social media in plain English. She helps entrepreneurs improve their online presence through webinars, workshops, presentations and consultations. Many of her training webinars are now video recordings posted on her website, and she uses videos on her blog and in her volunteer work.

Robin currently serves on the Pennsylvania PTA Board of Managers as a social media specialist and is a past president of the Pennsylvania Business Education Association. A sought-after trainer, speaker and consultant, she has spoken at state and national conferences and to an international audience through her online webinars. She is a founding member of the Global Social Media Managers Association™.

A wife and mother of a 16-year-old son, Robin enjoys spending time with her family, traveling, social networking, scrapbooking, reading, kayaking and zip lining. She is a volunteer at her son's school and with her church.

Let's Get Productive!

Move from Wasting Time and Being Overwhelmed to Being in Control

By Rosie Aiello, MBA

Do you ever wish you had more time? I mean, *really* have more time, where the day has 30 hours instead of 24? On the other hand, do you wish you could make time stop, like in the science fiction movies? Then, all those projects you are behind in—or never had time for—can finally be done?

We are stuck with 24 hours in which to live and manage our day. "Manage" is the operative word. If we misuse or waste time, we are throwing money out the door. Yes, it is as simple as that. Your profits are directly related to how well you manage your time.

Every small business owner has multiple tasks to manage: the work of your particular specialty (that is the reason you went into business), networking, writing blogs and e-zines, creating podcasts, maintaining a website, updating Facebook® and Twitter®, invoicing, paying bills, depositing checks at the bank, financial record management (such as

QuickBooks®), document filing, reading and responding to emails, telephone calls, Internet research, preparing and presenting speeches and workshops. It is enough to make you dizzy!

It is very clear that you are extremely busy! With all these tasks, it is no wonder we become overwhelmed, which makes the effective use of time even more critical.

The more organized you are, the greater are the possibilities for success. We often feel we need more time simply because our "to-do" list is unending. Sorry to say, that unending to-do list is never going to change. However, by creating systems to improve productivity throughout your business, you can get back in control and stop feeling overwhelmed.

Where Does Your Time Go and How to Manage It Better?

We are familiar with the saying, "Time flies when you're having fun." Time also flies when you are trying to manage your business. Unless you know where and how you are wasting your time, you will not know how to fix the problem. Let us review how all those hours are sapped and what you can do about it.

Interruptions and Distractions. How many times a day are you interrupted? Do you even realize you are being interrupted, or do you just assume it is part of doing business? The telephone rings. Your "You've-got-email" pings. Your spouse, partner, child or pet wanders into your office and wants attention. With today's economy, many small business owners work from home. Distractions and interruptions abound. A major study in 2006 by Dr. Gloria Mark of the University of California, Irvine, showed that every time someone is distracted, by a phone call for example, it takes more than 23 minutes to reset, refocus and get back to the task! If you have three interruptions a day, you have lost an hour of productive time. Your day spins out of control.

How to get back in control from interruptions and distractions:

- Block time on your calendar and return calls at your convenience.
- Do not automatically answer the telephone when it rings. Silence your cell phone. Let the answering service record the message. With caller ID, you can often identify the caller and judge how critical it is to take that call at that moment.
- Turn off the email arrival notice. If you are expecting an email within minutes, check your email when you are ready. (More on emails later.)
- Set boundaries with colleagues, spouses and children. This requires more diplomacy, especially if you do not want to end up sleeping on the sofa. By setting clear boundaries up front, confrontation and hurt feelings can be minimized. Sometimes, you might need to hang a notice on the outside of your door to indicate you are busy, such as a yellow note card to indicate you do not want to be disturbed. Colors are easy for small children to understand, too. Explain to others beforehand what the sign signifies and why you are placing it. Maintain the boundaries you have set.
- If you work at home, turn off the dryer or washing machine bell. Do laundry and other household chores during non-work hours.

Emails. Emails are a great communication tool if used and managed properly. How many emails do you receive in a day? How many e-newsletters? How often are you checking email? Do you feel obligated to check your email every few minutes?

How to get back in control with emails:

- In your calendar, set specific blocks of times during the day to check and read your email. For some, that may mean three times a day—30-minute periods in the morning, in the afternoon and before close of day. Randomly checking emails is a major source of interruption, breaking your train of thought, forcing your brain to reset and wasting time.

- Create a separate email account to receive e-newsletters and other subscriptions. There is no reason to clog your business email address with daily or weekly information. When you separate the critical information from the non-critical information, you can visually scan faster and address the important information more efficiently.
- Unsubscribe now to e-newsletters, coupon sites and any other e-data that you do not have time to read or are unable to search on the Internet.
- Set a specific time block on your calendar to read newsletters. E-newsletters can be printed or read on a digital reader. Plan to read while riding public transportation.
- Create file folders in your inbox for main topics—clients, prospects, follow-up, e-newsletters.
- Use the "Delete" button. Delete the original email immediately after you have replied or read an e-newsletter. Waiting until later will force you to reopen and remember what it was, wasting time.
- Immediately respond to emails that will take two minutes or less. For emails that require a longer response, create a separate time block on your calendar when you will reply.
- If you need to save the replies you send, create the option to have it filed immediately in the appropriate folder before you hit send. Outlook®, for example, has an "Options" tab where this can be done.
- For more important and frequently viewed email folders, start the name of the folder with the @ sign, which will bring the folder to the top. This will save you scanning time to reach the correct folder.
- Review the junk or spam folder frequently to avoid missing important emails that may have slipped in there. The smaller the list, the quicker you can scan and delete. I check mine almost daily. It takes a couple of seconds to scan and delete or move valid emails to the inbox.

Internet. Our society has added a new addiction: the Internet. How many times do you start to research something on the Internet, only to find yourself going deeper and deeper from link to link? As you close a site, a page pops up with some enticing news and gossip tidbits, written with an "I-can't-ignore-this" headline. I am good at controlling myself, and I still succumb to interest and curiosity, which ends up sending me on a trip that can last more than a couple of minutes. The incredible ease of data access has become a scourge of time. We need to develop a new willpower. A 2008 study by AOL® and Salary.com® show that about an hour a day is lost performing unnecessary tasks on the Internet. That equals five hours a week or six workweeks a year that are completely lost. When you are managing a small business, the direct hit to your profit line is significant.

How to get back in control with the Internet:

- Block the time on your calendar when you plan to research or read on the Internet.
- Use a timer to control how long you stay on the Internet. Most cell phones have a timer. You can also set an alarm to ring at a particular time. I use both, depending on the circumstance. If your cell phone does not have this feature, you can use a simple egg or kitchen digital timer. Using a timer keeps you focused.
- When you are tempted to click on a link out of curiosity, ask yourself, "By clicking on this link, am I helping my business or wasting time?" By challenging yourself, you will learn to become less tempted by the distractions of the Internet.
- Use a timer. Yes, I know I am repeating, but that is how critical it is to use one.
- Check out Internet tools, such as rescuetime.com®. When installed, this tool will track how much time you are spending on each website. You can also set a limit on how much time you want to spend on the Internet.

Paper. How much paper do you have on your desk—or on the floor? Barbara Hemphill, author of *Taming the Paper Tiger at Work,* from Kaplan Publishing in 2005, writes, "Clutter is postponed decisions."

Which is easier? Filing the document or just adding it to a stack? It takes time to file, especially if you do not have a good filing system. Adding it to a stack takes a second. However, how much time are you spending searching in the piles for that one document you saw several days ago? Several problems arise when papers are not managed in an effective manner. You waste an inordinate amount of time looking for the document. You feel stressed and frustrated because you cannot locate what you are looking for.

Paper clutter does not only occupy physical space, it also occupies visual space. When you have visual clutter, it is a drain on mental energy and productivity. When I sort clutter in an office, my clients feel a renewed sense of energy they did not even realize was being zapped by the disorder.

Although society is moving to using less paper, we are not yet completely paper *free.*

How to get back in control with paper:

- Block time on your calendar when you are going to handle incoming paper. Depending on your volume of paper, you may decide to have two blocks of time per day.
- Just as you scan for the importance of emails, do the same for paper. Recycle junk mail immediately.
- Create a hanging desk file to sort and manage incoming paper. **H**orizontal papers become **h**idden. **V**ertical files can be **v**iewed.
- Hanging desk file folders can include: Phone calls (notes of phone calls to make); Correspondence; Research (on-line); Bills (to pay);

To Scan (then recycle paper); Archive/To file—action taken, or reference material you want to keep.
- Block time on your calendar to handle all the subjects in your hanging file folders.
- Create a paper filing system that works for you and your business. The objective of filing is not to put it away, so it can no longer be seen. The goal is to retrieve it quickly when you want it. Think twice about why you are keeping that file. Most of what we keep, we never look at again. See the chapter "I Hate Paperwork" by Judy Rough on page 197.
- Scan and then recycle the paper.
- Maintain your file system. Go through your files at least annually and purge.

Computer Documents. As with paper documents, computer-generated documents can be lost unless a system is created to locate them quickly. Are you spending an excess amount of time trying to locate that document you wrote or saved on your hard drive?

Tags and keywords are great tools to help you zone in on the subject. What if you cannot remember the words that go with that exact document?

Scattered electronic documents create the same visual clutter as paper clutter, diminishing your mental energy.

How to get back in control with computer documents:

- Create file folders as you do with paper folders to narrow your search time.
- Group same subjects and topics together.
- Be consistent in your filing system, for example—File Folder: Clients. File name: Last Name, First Name, Company Name, Date.

For example: *Clients (Main Folder, equivalent to Pendaflex®) Ames, John, Acme Tools, 05.06.11 (equivalent to a manila file folder)*
- Choose file folder names that make sense for you and your business.
- On a quarterly or annual basis, block time on the calendar to purge data you have saved.

Business Boosters. I hope that you started your business because you love what you do—your expertise. However, you soon realized that running a business is much more than doing just what you love.

As I mentioned in the introduction, your day is replete with many activities besides performing tasks in your area of expertise. It is easy to slip into the "I-need-to-save-money-so-I'll-do-it-all-myself" syndrome. What happens, however, is that you spend more time performing activities that are beyond your knowledge and skill level and that take you away from your primary business goals. You waste time as you struggle to do everything yourself. You are inefficient because you do not know how to perform the particular task well, the task takes much more time than you originally thought, and the task often is not completed correctly. You end up with a triple whammy: lost time, poor outcome and stress.

How to get back in control with your expertise versus everything else:

- Identify and focus on your business goals and priorities. Look at them daily or at least weekly.
- Identify tasks where you need help or ones you do not like to perform. These will be the areas that will create procrastination and stagnation. Start to delegate those tasks to someone else. For example, hire a bookkeeper, a virtual assistant or a web designer.
- For those less-than-favorite tasks you decide you must manage yourself, block time on your calendar during a period when you have high energy and focus because you will need it!

- Realize where you are in the timeline of your business. Your needs will change as your business grows. Perhaps you created your own website to get started, and now it is time to step up and invest in something more professional that is designed by an expert.
- Invest in yourself and your business. Take professional development classes to improve yourself and strengthen your expertise. Invest in a marketing consultant, productivity consultant, business coach—or all three—to help you stay focused and to grow your business.

As we went through the different categories, you will have noticed a common theme to get back in control—*block time on your calendar.* When you are tempted to put something on your to-do list, ask yourself, "When am I going to do this?" Remember you need to manage your entire life—work, family, play, personal needs, spirituality and so on in each 24-hour period. When you plan time to perform a particular activity, you will be in control and feel more satisfied, plus it will more likely be accomplished.

You know the adage, "The bigger the house, the more you will fill it." I hope you realize by now that even if you had 30 hours in a day, and you did not have systems to manage your time, you would just fill it by doing "stuff."

When you are juggling many activities, the situation can become overwhelming. Add to that the need for a personal life, and you may wonder when there will ever be time for you.

The antidote to feeling stressed and overwhelmed in your business is to be in control, to put yourself back in the driver's seat, leading and directing instead of reacting. Start applying these tips, and you will not only have the satisfaction of empowerment, you will have more time to work on your business instead of in your business. You will create greater income-producing opportunities and achieve your success.

Rosie Aiello, MBA

Clearing the Path to Improved Small Business Productivity—More Time, Less Stress and Increased Profits
(415) 967-0571
Rosie@ClearVistaConsulting.com
www.ClearVistaConsulting.com

Rosie created ClearVista Consulting after a successful thirty-year career that started in Silicon Valley corporate finance. Her diverse experience with nonprofits, small businesses, event planning, and living and working internationally have given her the skills, knowledge and expertise to help small business owners become more organized and productive.

Working with busy, often overwhelmed, entrepreneurs who want to have less stress and more time to grow their business, Rosie is an expert at assessing a business owner's challenges. She develops processes and systems that run the business more effectively, increase profits, improve productivity and create better focus—all of which put busy people back in control.

Rosie does not know if she was born with an "organizing gene," learned it from her parents or developed the skill out of a necessity to excel in the corporate world. She does know she is passionate about helping people become more organized and productive to achieve greater success in their business. Her warm and friendly approach attracts even the most hesitant entrepreneurs who feel ashamed of their plight. Rosie is a member of the National Association of Professional Organizers®.

■ ■ ■

I Hate Paperwork!

If Papers Control Your Life, It Is Time to Control Your Papers—and All Those Emails!

By Judy Rough, CSA

Entrepreneurs spend much of their time at the ten-thousand-foot level. It is natural territory for them because in order to launch their business, they must have the vision, see the big picture and develop strategies and plans to realize their dreams. However, what about the paperwork? Most people, especially entrepreneurs, often hate paperwork. It is the bane of our existence! However, the world and business only work when you have good documentation that you can put your finger on in minutes.

The question is this: *How do we get control of something we actually do not want anything to do with?*

If it is within your budget, you might hire an assistant or a professional organizer to set up a document management system, or they might work to keep you organized and on task. You may also have a friend or associate who will act as an accountability partner, or if you have the time, you can commit to just do it yourself.

Before you decide which direction to take, you need to think about the pain that exists in your life from the chaos of your paper—both hardcopy and virtual. Were you looking for the copy of your current business license and came across your child's immunization record? Were you trying to keep on top of business receipts and sent a receipt from Victoria's Secret® to the accountant, which resulted in questions about whether you had added a new revenue stream to your business?

Time is a very precious commodity, and when we spend time looking for a physical piece of paper that is missing or an electronic document that is lost somewhere on our hard drive, we become frustrated, and our stress level soars.

When you own a home-based business or work from home, is the line blurred between maintaining and separating your business records from your personal documents? Maybe the time has come to try a new approach that will prevent confusion between your business and personal paper life and be the key to your sense of overall organization, thus giving yourself the gift of time and peace of mind.

What's Your Style?

Are you most like one of the following five types? Are you ready to stop procrastinating and take control? Read the description and decide which type is most closely like you.

Type 1. Always in control of my paper and electronic records and documents.

- I can find almost any paper or electronic file I need in five minutes or less.
- If I were unexpectedly delayed returning home from a business trip, my trusted representative would have all the information necessary to take care of affairs until I returned.

- I have communicated everything my agents need to know about my business records.
- I generally feel relaxed and prepared for tax time.
- I know exactly what I own, who will inherit it and where it is.
- I have thought through and formalized my buy/sell agreement and end of life wishes and plans.
- I am sure everything is up to date.
- I have a review process in place.

Type 2. Sometimes (or used to be) in control of my records and important documents.

- I am generally an organized person when it comes to my business, except when life throws a curve ball at me.
- I still manage to meet day-to-day demands and to keep on top of bills, taxes and papers, and I have a good credit.
- I constantly think about making my estate plans, and I am afraid I don't have the documents in order to even go to the attorney,
- I do want to be in control of the important things, and the thought of trying to be perfectly organized is overwhelming,
- I am not sure what I need to keep and what I can shred.
- I do not have a system for keeping my user IDs and passwords at hand, and I am always wasting time finding them.

Type 3. Need to get in control of my records and documents.

- I spend my life searching for missing or misplaced things.
- The papers in my life are in chaos.
- The only way I find out I owe a bill is when I get the overdue notice.
- My credit is poor.
- I am never ready for tax time and I have no idea where many of my receipts are.

- I feel I am drowning in responsibility.
- I have no plans for emergencies or my future financial life.
- I would get my papers and plans in order if I knew how.
- I have not decided who will manage my affairs in my absence.
- I tend to procrastinate and put off these things until I am forced into it.

Type 4. Never had to be in control of my own papers and plans.

- I have suddenly become responsible for all of my papers and plans.
- I do not know where to begin.
- I am not very computer savvy.
- I know planning is critical.
- I want to be an informed decision-maker about my business future and legacy.

Type 5. Want to start my new business in control of my affairs.

- I am in the startup phase of my business and I want to avoid the paper drama I see everyone coping with today.
- I am at a loss as to what is important to keep and what I can pitch.
- I want to take responsibility now.
- I want to spend a little time now and save a lot of time later.
- I am a digital person, and I want to make sure I have the paper copies I need.
- I have no system in place to hold my records and documents or my current receipts and tax papers.
- I would like to understand what is coming up the road that I will need in terms of papers and planning.
- I hate to waste time searching for critical records and documents.
- I loose or forget my user IDs and passwords often.

Here is a simple approach that can get you organized by using electronic folders and one or several binders in addition to or instead of files. Once you have committed to this or another system of organization, do not forget to delegate these tasks, whenever possible. As an entrepreneur, you can design the approach and instruct an assistant to work with you to customize a unique system that works best with your business and style of working.

Take Control

The following steps will provide you with control over the dreaded paperwork:

Step #1: Create a roadmap of your new organization system—one that can be helpful to you and can be easily communicated to your trusted representative. This roadmap is simply a list of the categories you wish to catalogue, such as legal, financial, insurance, taxes, estate planning, equipment and supplies, marketing and so on.

Every business has its own unique requirements and unique set of documents beyond the standard finance, license and tax-related papers. Take the time to talk to your professionals, search online or contact the small business administration in your area for details on documentation and records required for your type of business or industry.

Some common examples are:

- Accounts list
- Advertising
- Bank records / statements
- Articles of incorporation
- Printed materials
- Budget

- Business license
- Business plan
- Contacts
- Credit / debit cards
- Employer Identification Number (EIN)
- Expense tracking
- Insurance
- Keys and access codes
- Legal
- Marketing plan
- Marketing materials
- Passwords
- Professional memberships
- Receipts
- Reseller's license
- Tax records
- Website

Step #2: Make a list of all the records and documents you want to put into each category. The list of categories and the list of documents can be ever changing—just add or delete, as needed.

On your list of records and documents, indicate where each item is located, such as within the binder, in a file, in a safe deposit box and so on. This location information is invaluable for your trusted representative in the event of your incapacity or other emergency. Many people do this for their personal records, and it is surprising how many neglect to consider business records or business life.

Step #3: Collect your records and documents and put them into sheet protectors in the correct category in your binder. You may wish to consider labeling each document for quick identification. If you are unable to locate these documents, or if you need to create or replace a document, it is a good idea to create a place for them and add them to your list. Simply indicate the item is being created or you have ordered a replacement. Also, put a blank sheet protector within the correct category with a label on the upper right corner of the sheet protector that shows the name of the document for that spot. In this way, you have a running to-do list in your binder, and your trusted representative will know the status.

Step #4: Indicate which documents need reviewing or updating, such as your insurance coverage. As you are putting items in place, you may wish to scan each document and go digital. This creates an excellent backup for your paper records.

When you store your scanned documents in electronic folders, make sure to label each folder to match the categories in your binder and ensure consistency and ease of use. Your professionals can advise what you need to keep in paper form. Creating digital documents may reduce the amount of paper you have to store in your binder system.

Step #5: Once your system is established, be sure to find a location in your home that is separate from your personal papers. Be aware of security and protection against theft, fire and so on. Consider using a safe deposit box, safe or fireproof box for physical items, and be sure you are backing up and properly storing your electronic files using an external drive, disc, encrypted software and so on. You may wish to have electronic backup copies of your records and documents stored off-site using the Internet cloud.

Step #6: Tell your trusted representative where all the records and documents are stored and be sure they have access, if needed. Remember to include an extra set of keys for your representative or any other item it would be important for them to have access to. Make sure they also have login and user IDs for remote digital storage solutions.

Step #7: Set a recurring appointment on your calendar to do a once-a-year review and update of your system and records. Think of it as "spring cleaning." No more outdated or missing records and documents. You are in control.

You now have a grab-and-go system for use in an emergency or in the event of a disaster. Your binder is a handbook for daily use in your business and allows you and anyone you are working with to be highly efficient and productive. You will not waste time searching for lost items or trying to remember where you filed something.

Step #8: Once you have collected all of the physical records and documents required to run and maintain your business, you are ready to go digital. Refer back to Step #1 and for all the categories you have established in your binder system, and you will duplicate those categories as electronic folders on your computer.

Now, you can scan records and documents from your binder and file them electronically in the correct folder on your computer. For example, you may have your paper copy of the *Articles of Incorporation* physically filed under the category called "Legal." You can scan the *Articles* or request an electronic copy from your attorney and file them in an electronic folder called "Legal." You will file any future legal documents in this folder as well as any emails that you wish to keep that are under the legal category.

You can speak with your professionals to determine which documents require a paper copy. For those records and documents that do not require the physical paper version, going digital will greatly reduce the volume of physical paper to control. As with paper files, you must schedule regular electronic file reviews to delete outdated or unnecessary items.

Reaching Papervana

Remember, if papers control your life, it is time to control your physical papers as well as your electronic ones. Do not wait another minute. Just start with one document, and you will be better off than you were the day before. Be successful and manage this project one step at a time at your own pace. This is not an overwhelming task.

How do you eat an elephant?

One bite at a time.

Your goal is to reach the state of *Papervana.*

Papervana*—noun [paper-vah-nuh]—a place or state of freedom from pain, suffering or worry related to one's piles and files of records and documents.*

You are now in control of keeping only the records and documents that are needed, and you have a clear roadmap to be used in your estate planning. This is a blessing for your trusted representatives and loved ones. Leaving a legacy that is in order reduces the burden left for those dealing with your estate.

You can show up for work in your home office dressed professionally from the waist up ready for that meeting using Skype®, and from the waist down dressed, comfortably in your yoga pants with your bunny slippers tapping happily under the desk. Your papers are in order, your plans are in place, and your life is more at ease. Feel the positive ripple effect when you commit to taking back control.

Judy Rough, CSA

Papervana™, LLC

If papers control your life,
it's time to control your papers

(480) 200-3415
judy@papervana.com
www.papervana.com

With decades of experience in vital record and document organizing, Judy Rough, home downsizing expert and senior move manager, is passionate about helping clients get their ducks in a row to escape their paper drama. Her user-friendly insightful approach to helping people organize their life's papers and plans has made her a sought-after coach, workshop leader and speaker at national conferences.

Judy is owner of Carefree Transitions™, LLC, a move management and record and document-organizing firm in Scottsdale, Arizona. A member of the National Association of Senior Move Managers™ (NASMM), she was honored with the organization's Circle of Service Award. Judy is also a member of the National Association of Professional Organizers™ (NAPO) and holds the NAPO Golden Circle Membership designation. She has a certification from the Society of Certified Senior Advisors™ (CSA).

Judy is the creator of the Papervana system, an online tutorial for the organizing and managing life's papers and plans, and the owner of Papervana, LLC, which is the culmination of Judy's lifetime passion to help bring order and peace of mind to our complex lives—just one step at a time.

■ ■ ■

Quarterbacking Without Touching the Ball

Build Winning Teams by Transitioning from a Doer to a Leader

By Felicia Streeter, MBA

In my experience as co-founder of Streeter Construction Group and my one-on-one work with entrepreneurs to mentor them on how to grow a million-dollar business, I have learned that many businesses don't make it to their five-year anniversary and, unfortunately, even fewer make it to the million-dollar profit mark.

Why? I have discovered it is usually the back office that makes most businesses crumble.

Many entrepreneurs—especially those with back office problems—have a problem letting go. They want to be involved in every aspect of their business because they have a mistaken belief that no one can do it as good as they can. They do not trust their team. Most entrepreneurs are too attached to their businesses. They treat the business like their children.

If you want to grow a million-dollar business, this chapter will give you the key to building a team of independent contractors, employees or partners to accomplish your goal of making more money and working less. As the business owner, you have to be the thought leader. You have to create the vision, communicate it to your team and rest assured that the various tasks to achieve it will be completed.

As the visionary, your job is to work *on* the business and not *in* the business. This is sometimes confusing. It means that when you are working in your business, you are doing things that could be outsourced or that your employees should be doing. Some of these tasks might include posting to your accounting software, updating your website or any other day-to-day task that involves basic administration.

On the other hand, working *on* your business is where you are the quarterback, and you are throwing the ball to your tight end or wide received. Of course, you have options based on the play you are running. You are leading your team, and you are passing the ball. At that point, you have a hands-off approach. You know you can trust that wide receiver or tight end to run the ball for a touchdown. This is you as the quarterback communicating the vision and then passing the task to the wide receiver or tight end.

If you have to touch or be involved with everything that goes on in your business, and no one has the authority to approve anything without you, you are no longer an entrepreneur—you have become your own employee!

What happens if you have to have your hand in everything that goes on? You have to sign all documents.

What happens when you are out of town, and you have to touch everything and put your stamp of approval on it? Will that document sit on your desk until you return to the office?

What impact will your absence have on your business? Will invoices and employees be paid when you are gone?

What happens after a job or an assignment ends? You do not have another job lined up because you were working on the previous job instead of looking for more work and marketing your business.

Your objective should be to bring in the work and let your team execute and complete the work. That is the quarterback passing the ball. Do not let your back office prevent the success in your front office. Both areas are equally important.

What is preventing you from letting go of the ball? Is it a lack of systems, resources, communication problems or an inability to let go and delegate?

Ready to quarterback without touching the ball? There are five steps:

1. Pitch your vision.
2. Create a structure to support your business.
3. Keep your eye on the ball.
4. Get first-and-tens.
5. Get out of the huddle and into action!

Pitch Your Vision

In order to grow your business, the first thing you must have is a vision. What is your path? What do you want to accomplish in the next 12 months? What is your business model, mission, vision, revenue goals—everything you want to accomplish? Clearly state the ultimate outcome. Once you are clear, you can share the vision with your team.

Here are a few steps you can implement to have your team see the vision just as you do.

- Get clarity on what you offer...your service or product.
- What are your sales goals—make sure you cover your expenses, your salary, and profit and this number should be a bit of a stretch.
- Why are you in business.
- What is the result of what you do.
- What you want for your team—the result for them too because you want them to be vested also.

It is time to meet with your key personnel, internal and external. As the visionary, you have to get them to buy into the vision and commit to the company, the mission and your vision. For maximum results, work has to be more than just a paycheck for them.

You can offer your team all, a few, or a variety of incentives like:

- Monetary bonus
- Award recognition
- Appreciation gift certificates
- Send them referrals

Create a Structure to Support Your Business

As the quarterback, you need four things in place before you can pass the ball and be assured your team can carry it to the goal.

- Systems
- Automation
- Delegation
- Team building

You have to ensure each of these things are in place for your business to grow and thrive. If you do not, you will go from overwhelm to distress to burnout, and you will want to quit. Remember, it is not a job. It is your business. You cannot just call in tomorrow and quit.

So dig in and let us get to work. Let's put in place the process needed to quarterback without touching the ball.

Systems. Streamlining your systems within your business is vital. I know you have the systems for your business.

There are three key systems you are probably doing and do not realize that you are:

1. Invoicing customers

2. Fulfilling your services and/or orders

3. Over all operation of your business

Maybe you have systems, but they are in your head. Let's take them out of your head and get them on paper. Have a family member, friend or your assistant take notes while you describe the steps of each system within your business. You can commit to formalizing one system a week until you get them all out of your head and on to paper.

Ask someone that does not know the system to review it to find any gaps in flow and understanding. Have them ask questions in areas they do not understand. Then you can fill in the gaps and have a system that anyone can implement. See "Let's Get Productive!" by Rosie Aiello on page 187.

Automation. This is where you will use technology. There is a lot of software available now, and more is being created daily to allow you to automate your business. For example, following up with your clients might be something you would like to implement. This is where most fall short. Most shopping carts and customer relationship manager software (CRM) allow you to automate your follow up.

Find software that will allow you to automate your follow up to stay connected with your database on a regular basis.

There are many different types of software available to you as a small business owner. It can be very confusing if you are not clear on what you need to operate your business more effectively, but on a small business budget.

Low cost and effective software I suggest my clients use starting out are:

- **1Shopping Cart**. Used to allow customers to purchase products or services from your website.
- **High Rise**. Customer relationship manager used for storing contacts and taking notes.
- **Audio Acrobat**. Used to record audios for products, website, or sessions with clients.
- **Constant Contact**. Used for email marketing and capturing contact information of people opting-in on your website.
- **Free Conference Pro**. Used to hold conference calls—can be with two people or multiple people.

In selecting your software, you want to think of ease of use, cost and the ability to automate. That way you are saving money and getting more time back.

Delegation. Do not cringe. It will be okay. This is another vital key to making more, working less and having more fun. This is where you have the hands off approach. Let's say you're overwhelmed and have too much on your plate, yet you won't delegate! You think no one can do it as good as you, it will not be on time, and the list goes on. It is time you shift your mindset. If you have an effective team and understand each person's abilities and skillset, it will be easier for you to delegate.

Maybe you do not know what to delegate. Make a list of the following:

1. Things you don't like to do
2. Things you don't do and need to do
3. Things you do and don't want to do

You now have a list of things you can delegate. I would suggest starting with the things that are not getting done and then the things you do not want to do.

Now, you will want to make a list of all the things you do in your business and at home. Take maybe seven days to track what you are doing.

- Categorize the list by importance.
- Describe your process—the steps it takes to complete each item.
- Interview prospects based on the task delegating and their skill-set.
- Make your selection.

Team Building. This is quarterbacking at its best. Your team is now effective because you have systems in place you are automating and delegating.

Some entrepreneurs make a mistake in thinking that one person will solve all their problems and can do it all. This is not the case. As you build your team, whether they are independent contractors, employees or virtual assistants, be sure to make your selection based on skillset as it relates to what you plan to achieve. See "Hiring the Right People" by Cynthia Fassler on page 217.

Keep Your Eye on the Ball

As the task (project) is moving through the departments, the team is working with the processes and systems you have implemented. You can see timely workflow and know things are being completed.

Competency and capabilities are everything. If you do not like how a particular task is being handled, do not just step in. There is more than one way to get things done. The goal is the result, right? So keep your hands off the task and do not micromanage. That will only get you working more, and the objective is to work less.

You do want updates weekly or more, if needed. Communicate your expectations, goals, timeline, urgency, and anything that will help your team be successful in completing the mission. Even if you have a virtual team, you can meet regularly since the technology is available via voice or video. This is where you want to have your hand on the task and be firm. Hold those meetings.

Get First and Tens

During the course of meetings or if someone tells you that things are off course, you may need to step in. Remember, your team is there to handle the day-to-day operations. When there are obstacles this is where you, the visionary, need to change the play and/or change the players. Get things back on track, so you can get to the next first-and-ten and keep forward movement to the goal.

Ultimately, you reach your goal. You have completed the order or provided the service, delivered the product on schedule and within budget.

You have scored a touchdown.

Get Out of the Huddle and into Action!

Over the next thirty days, you can get your systems out of your head and on paper for your team. Automating your systems using technology will provide you more time. Create your delegation checklist of what tasks you are going to delegate and to what skill-set you will want to bring on your team.

Congratulations! You are ready to quarterback without touching the ball!

Get out there, make more money, work less, have more time and lots more fun.

Felicia Streeter, MBA

Dream4self, Inc.

The Million-Dollar Mentor: Make More Money, Find More Time, Work Less, and Have More Fun

(214) 295-4332

Felicia@feliciastreeter.com

www.feliciastreeter.com

Felicia Streeter, co-founder of Streeter Construction Group, author and speaker, works one-on-one with entrepreneurs mentoring them on how to grow a million-dollar business. She specializes in building streamlined systems and effective teams and in leveraging time. This gives her clients strategies, tools and a plan of action to transition from a "doer" to a leader and grow their business fast.

Felicia's passion is sharing her knowledge, lessons learned and the strategies she used to take her business from $23,000 to over $7,000,000 in 18 months!

Felicia has a master of business administration in entrepreneurship and strategic management, a bachelor of arts in management and an associate bachelor of arts in accounting from Davenport University. Her experience includes seven years entrepreneurship, fifteen years with the federal government and ten years as a military spouse, traveling in the United States and abroad. She is uniquely qualified to develop programs and mentor entrepreneurs on growing their business.

Hiring the Right People

By Cynthia Fassler

When you are a solo entrepreneur and are doing it all, there comes a time when you need to stop working in your business and start working on your business. Burn out can be costly. When you are ready to grow your business, you may need to bring on help to take you to the next level. You may already have had employees in a variety of roles to help build your company or to keep the company moving in the right direction. When the workload overwhelms the workforce, you get diminishing returns on productivity and morale. Do not overwork your core team—start thinking about hiring additional staff to keep things moving smoothly.

Hiring the right person is your goal. You will incur costs for recruiting, benefits, training and salary, and you want a return on your investment. Good hires improve morale, productivity and confidence in management. On the other hand, bad hires can damage your business's reputation.

Have a plan ready and ask yourself the following questions to make sure that you are happy with your answers.

What am I looking for? The answer should be about the big picture. It is going to be the framework around which you will build your plan. Think in general terms. "I want to grow my business to five employees." "I need to have my marketing department built by the end of the year." In other words, broad term goals for where you want to take your company.

Who am I looking for? A worker bee, a visionary, a degreed professional? This is where you need to figure out the particular qualifications and personality of the person you want to bring onto the team. Let's say you're looking to fill out your marketing department. Do you already have an expert graphics engineer? Is the missing piece the brilliant idea maker? Perhaps you need a no-nonsense manager to keep all those creative minds working in the same direction. Think about your company as a puzzle. Every piece is a necessary part of the whole, and each piece is unique. Figure out the shape of the piece that is missing.

It is fine to hire someone to just get things done, like someone to pay your bills or someone who has an expertise that you do not possess—like a graphic designer—to head up your rebranding.

How am I going to locate the right person? You have multiple options here—online job boards, job fairs and college career centers. You can work through your network and look for a referral. Working with a recruiter is also an option.

Online job boards are great if you want to fill a reasonably common position, such as receptionist, junior-level administrative assistant, bookkeeper or human resource assistant. You have many options. Monster.com™, Careerbuilder.com™ and Craigslist.org™ are three great resources for a broad spectrum of disciplines. There are also many smaller specialized job boards. You will get a flood of resumes from candidates that are, hopefully, qualified to do the job you need. The downside to this option is that you will also get numerous resumes from people who are simply blasting their resumes out to any and every job posting. This option has the potential to be the most time-consuming. If you are going to post on the Internet, figure out how much time you will be willing to spend reviewing resumes.

Job fairs are another option, and are a time- and resource-intensive undertaking. If it is a good job fair, you will find many eager, qualified job candidates. This option is best if you have someone to attend the job fair with you, so that candidates do not become impatient while waiting to tell you why you should hire them.

College career centers are great for finding an entry-level person who possesses a specific knowledge set. For example, if you are working on building your marketing department and branding and design functions, contacting the career center at an art school is a great way to reach candidates with a degree in graphic design who are knowledgeable about current trends.

Reaching out to your network for a referral offers many advantages. You will have a solid base on which to build a complete picture of the candidates. Perhaps an old colleague who is now a CFO can give you the names of some great accountants with whom they have worked. Personal referrals are the best recommendation you can receive.

The advantages of working with a recruiter are varied. They are the experts in hiring, identifying, qualifying and delivering the perfect match for the job. This is a great option if you are in a time crunch or are looking for a specific type of employee. Most recruiters have a pool of candidates they can quickly consider and identify a match for your requirements.

Recruiters have a system they use to identify candidates who match your qualifications. The candidates have been interviewed, skills assessed and background checked. Recruiters are also great for finding that needle-in-the-haystack candidate, such as a tax accountant who has international tax experience and happens to be a CPA with fifteen years of experience. Another advantage is that recruiters can offer you temporary or temp-to-hire candidates if you are still unsure about jumping into the deep end of the hiring process.

What are the actual qualifications I need in an employee? One of the biggest mistakes entrepreneurs make is not knowing the true requirements of the position that they are hiring for. Write out the functions needed in a detailed job description. In addition to the job description, ask yourself what you want this person to be able to contribute to the company. Think about everything that you hope to have this person accomplish.

Your job description should have the following components to it:

- Title of the position.
- General job function and company background. Give the potential applicant a broad idea of what the position entails as well as what the company does. Another good thing to mention here is the culture of the company.
- Responsibilities. Go into detail about the expectations.
- Essential skills are the must-haves in the job.

- Qualifications. List any degrees or certifications and any specific software knowledge and experience that you require. The years of experience should also be listed here.
- Salary and benefits. Give the potential applicant an idea of what they can expect in the form of compensation. It is a waste of your time and theirs if your budget is $65K and they are looking for $85K.

Sample Job Description

Senior Accountant

Your Company—San Francisco, CA

General Job and Company Background

The Senior Accountant will report to the Assistant Controller and will be responsible for managing the process and reconciling the activity associated with Order to Cash Cycle and the related GL accounts. This position will work with other members in Accounting as well as with stakeholders from Product, Customer Service and Data Warehouse, to continuously review/identify issues/changes in the Order to Cash process to provide timely reports, as well as participate in ad hoc projects as required. This position will also manage a staff accountant to help in the billing, collections and payment applications.

Responsibilities

Perform monthly and quarterly activities in support of the financial close process including importing and exporting data, analyzing and explaining variances from expectations and reconciling associated general ledger accounts.

Coordinate process and reconcile monthly revenue close, including preparation and review of journal entries and account reconciliations for revenue, accounts receivable, deferred revenue, customer deposits and charge-back/returns.

Ensure accurate scheduling and recording of all revenue-related transactions in accordance with US Generally Accepted Accounting Principles (GAAP).

Assist internal customers to resolve issues/questions on activities related to Order to Cash cycle and the associated GL accounts.

Oversee invoicing and collection activities.

Work with Accounting Manager to ensure updated VAT rates stated in billing system for applicable sales areas.

Lead efforts to continuously drive cross-functional improvements associated with processes related to revenue-related reporting. Research and resolve reconciliation issues and discrepancies; take corrective measures to mitigate while enhancing procedures to prevent recurrence.

Support external audit activities and audit preparation.

Provide management with financial reporting information and operational support.

Essential Skills

Three to five years of progressive experience in corporate accounting; three years of public accounting experience; two years of audit experience.

Reporting to the audit committee.

Able to document accounting practices in accordance to GAAP.

Excellent analytical and Microsoft Excel® skills.

Qualifications
Bachelor's degree in accounting.

CPA certification is preferred.

Salary and Benefits
$70,000 to $80,000 Depending on Experience
Medical, Dental and Vision: Employee pays one-third and employer pays two-thirds of premium
401k after first year of employment

When do I need to have this position filled? Now that you have a better idea of whom, what and where you are looking, this is the time to figure out your time frame. Do you have to fill this position immediately or do you have some wiggle room? Can you set aside time from your other duties to focus on the search? Ask yourself, "Can I afford to not hire right now?" Your answer will be your determining factor as to what you need to do.

What is my time worth? Remember that time is money. Once you have made the decision on the type of employee you need, review your budget to see how much you can afford to spend on this new addition to your firm. Include salary, benefits, hiring and on-boarding costs. It might mean that you start with a junior person before you hire an expert.

How do I identify the perfect candidate? You have gotten a slew of responses to an online ad or the call to your network for referrals. There is a stack of resumes sitting on your desk, and you have no idea where to start. Here are some tips on how to make it a less daunting task. Have your hiring criteria handy, so you do not waste time reading the entire resume.

Hiring Criteria While Reviewing a Resume

A resume should be a snapshot of someone's work accomplishments—job title, stable work history, job function, location. The job function should be in line with your job description.

Read the resume for grammar and spelling. Someone who does not take time to proof his or her resume is not a detail-oriented person.

Select the top five submissions and start telephone screening to:

- Evaluate communication skills.
- Ask why they responded to your job posting.
- Find out if they are articulate when describing their capabilities.
- Answer any questions about the job.
- Confirm their asking salary.

Personal Interview

Create a list of questions that you will ask all of the applicants during the interview process. Here is a list of example questions that are a good base to work from.

- Reason you are looking for work?
- Provide me with a typical day in your last job?
- What kind of employee are you? One that saves the company money or that spends money to make the company more efficient?
- What stresses you out in your job?
- What would your last boss say about you?
- Why should I consider hiring you for this position?
- What do you know about our company?

Decision Time

After you have completed each interview, take time to ask yourself these questions and make a note of your answers. Also, keep track of your initial reaction to the interview and candidate.

- Is the candidate likeable, and would this person fit into our culture?
- Were they a good listener, did they pay attention to what you were saying or did they talk too much?
- Do you feel confident that they can do the job?
- Did what they said during the interview seem to match up with what is on their resume?

Remember that attitude and intuition is half of the hiring process.

Final Steps

Once you have made your selection, be sure to check at least two work references. It is often useful to get a reference from both an immediate supervisor as well as a professional colleague. While a supervisor can give you an indication of how successful the person was in his or her position, a colleague can give you insight into the person's work ethic and style.

If a degree or certification is required for your position, hire a background check firm to conduct a credit, criminal and educational background check. Here are some background check firms that have a great reputation: HireRight® (www.hireright.com), EmployeeScreenIQ® (www.employeescreen.com) or Intellius® (www.intelius.com) just to name a few.

Keep in mind that there are different laws regarding what you can or cannot use in the determination to hire a candidate in regards to their credit history and criminal background. If you are unsure about the regulations and laws in your own area, check with an attorney who is familiar with your state's legislation on this topic.

It is considered standard policy to extend an offer in writing. In your offer letter, outline the job title, job description, start date, salary and the benefits being offered. Always add a dual signature page. I believe all offers should be extended verbally first to give the new hire a warm personal welcome to your company and let them know that a written offer letter will follow.

I hope that in the interviewing process you had a secondary candidate whom you interviewed who was almost just as good a choice as your primary. Hold off on sending a rejection letter to that candidate. If your primary candidate declines your offer, you do not have to go through the entire process all over again. You can just pick up the phone and call your runner-up.

I always believe in personally contacting all of the runner-up candidates and letting them know that the choice was difficult and that we have selected a candidate who has accepted our offer. I then always wish them well in their search. If the decision was a close one, then consider asking the runner-ups whether they would be slighted by a call if the primary choice falls through.

As an owner or hiring manager, choosing the right person is one of the most critical things for your reputation and it will shape the confidence that your team will have in you. The right hire can help you take your business to the next level.

Hiring is not an exact science. It spans the globe of emotions. Step out of the emotional part and do what you would advise one of your colleagues to do when they have told you they are ready to expand their company. Make the decision on who would be the best person for your company.

Remember your vision and the reason you are ready to hire.

Happy interviewing!

Cynthia Fassler

TSS Total Staffing Solutions, Inc.

(415) 543-4545
cynthia@tssjobs.com
www.tssjobs.com

Cynthia Fassler founded TSS Total Staffing Solutions, Inc. in 1982 and it quickly expanded to fulltime placement and executive search. Known for her energetic style and commitment to customer satisfaction, Cindy is a recruiter who listens to her clients and finds top talent to meet their needs.

With a strong commitment to giving back to the community, Cindy shares her expertise to benefit other organizations. She served on the board of Jobs' Consortium and made it possible for the organization to open up an internal staffing service to place graduates. She also taught resume writing and job trends at City College of San Francisco and worked for the San Francisco Welfare-to-Work Program coaching re-entry workers on how to get a job.

Cindy is associated with and recognized by regional and national associations in her field. She received the Shero Award from the National Association of Personnel Services and was named the small business owner of the year in 2006, the highest award of esteem given by the Small Business Network. She was the statewide vice president of the California Staffing Professionals.

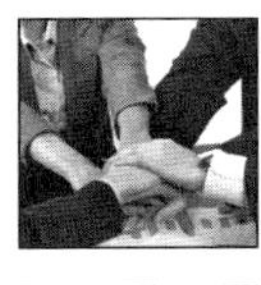

■ ■ ■

More Entrepreneur Extraordinaire

Now that you have learned many things about how to become a successful entrepreneur with a wide variety of tips, techniques and strategies, the next step is to take action. Get started applying what you have learned in the pages of this book.

We want you to know that we are here to help you meet your professional and personal objectives. Below is a list of where we are geographically located. Regardless of where our companies are located, many of us provide a variety of services over the phone or through webinars, and we welcome the opportunity to travel to your location.

You can find out more about each of us by reading our bios at the end of our chapters, or by visiting our websites listed on the next pages. When you are ready for one-on-one consulting or group training from any of the co-authors in this book—we are available! If you call us and let us know you have read our book, we will provide you with a free phone consultation to determine your needs and how we can best serve you.

United States

New York

Nilda Perez	www.aspire4life.com

California

Rosie Aiello	www.clearvistaconsulting.com
Elizabeth Bachman	www.befabuloustraining.com
Cynthia Bruno	www.humeglobalenterprises.com
Tamara Cameron	www.health-harvest.com
April P. Cooper	www.executivevpa.com
Alesia Dowden	www.alesiadowden.com
Cindy Fassler	www.tssjobs.com
Dortha Hise	www.dorthahise.com
Dakota McKenzie	www.dakotamacenzie.com
Caterina Rando	www.caterinarando.com
Judy Rough	www.papervana.com
Susan Rueppel	www.chiefintuitionofficer.com
Alexis Williams-Patton	www.alexiswilliamspattonenterprises.com

Florida

LeTonya F. Moore www.oppcoach.com

Washington

Brenda Lee Gallatin www.coach4successnow.com

Pennsylvania

Robin O'Neal Smith www.besocialgetsuccess.com

Texas

Kym Glass www.kymglass.com

Felicia Streeter www.feliciastreeter.com

Karen Terry www.fulltimewoman.com

Canada

Alberta

Win Day www.creativeimplementations.com

You're Invited...

. . .to join us for the **Business Breakthrough Summit** designed to give you tools to catapult your business growth.

The Business Breakthrough Summit is the right program for you if you want to create new streams of income, are ready to establish yourself as an expert in your field and are looking for a way of easily doing both. It is time for you to be one of the influential people in your field.

Join us at the Business Breakthrough Summit and in one weekend, you will gain the information and tools you need to accelerate your ability to easily add clients and learn how to be loud and proud about the value you bring to the marketplace.

Find out more about our next live event at: www.bizbreakthrough.com. Because you picked up and read this book, it is clear you have business savvy, therefore we have a gift for you. Enter coupon code BBSVIP50 for a 50% discount on your registration. Attend this event and watch your business thrive!

You're Invited...

. . .to join us for any of our **Sought After Speaker Summits!**

Do you have a message you want to share?
Are you ready to improve your speaking skills?
Have you seen how much influence people who speak have?
Would you like be a sought-after speaker?

In one weekend you can develop your public speaking skills and be loud and proud about the value you bring. Join us for our next live event at: www.soughtafterspeaker.com

Because you are savvy enough to pick up this book we have a gift for you. Enter coupon code SASVIP50 for a 50% discount on your registration. Attend this event and watch how your social status climbs!

Become a Published Author with THRIVE Publishing™

THRIVE Publishing develops books for experts who want to share their knowledge with more and more people. We can help you become a published author to showcase your expertise, build your list and advance your business and career.

We realize that getting a book written and published is a huge undertaking, and we make that process as easy as possible. We have an experienced team of professionals with the resources and knowledge to put a quality, informative book in your hands quickly and affordably.

We also partner with organizations or institutions to publish books that would be of interest to their members. In this case, sales of the book can be a revenue stream/fundraiser for the organization. A book can enhance your mission, give you a professional outreach tool and enable you to communicate essential information to a wider audience.

Contact us to discuss how we can work together
on *your* book project.

Phone: **415-668-4535**
email: **info@thrivebooks.com**

Also from THRIVE Publishing™

For more information
on this book, visit
www.womanentrepreneurbook.com

■ ■ ■

For more information
on this book, visit
www.incrediblebusinessbook.com

Also from
THRIVE Publishing™

For more information
on this book, visit
www.savvyleadership.com

■ ■ ■

For more information
on this book, visit
www.getorganizedtodaybook.com

Also from THRIVE Publishing™

For more information
on this book, visit
www.makeyourconnectionscount.com

■ ■ ■

For more information
on this book, visit
www.momentrepreneurbook.com

Also from THRIVE Publishing™

For more information
on this book, visit
www.execetiquette.com

■ ■ ■

For more information
on this book, visit
www.impact-pro.ca

Also from THRIVE Publishing™

For more information
on this book, visit
www.latinnovating.com

■ ■ ■

For more information
on this book, visit
www.secretstostayinginspired.com

Notes

Notes

Notes

Notes

Notes

For more copies of this book, *Entrepreneur Extraordinaire,* contact any of the co-authors or visit www.eetelesummit.com